THE PRAYING COWBOY

Leading Men To Christ Your Identity

JEFF W. RIPPY

ISBN (Paperback): 979-8-9881073-3-0
ISBN (eBook): 979-8-9881073-2-3

This book is dedicated to the memory of Pastor Rex Townsley.

January 1, 1960 – January 8, 2017

Contents

A man who touched so many lives: a person could feel God when they talked with Rex. In the brief time I knew Rex, he had a substantial influence on my life. I thank God for the time with him and his fellowship.

"Now death is not the worst thing that could happen to me because I will live forever in heaven. You see, my prayer is that you will choose Christ too. Then I will never say farewell to you."
Written by Rex

A Note to my Family

First, I want to thank my family for their support and love. A special thanks to my beautiful wife, Kim, who has been the love of my life for 43 years, my partner, best friend, and the mother of our four children. Thank you, honey, for never giving up on me during the tough times and always being there when we needed you the most. Thank you for your courage and determination leading me to the Lord, and never giving up on me.

The Reason For Writing This Book

Several years ago, God gave me a vision to author a book to help spread the word to men, women, and children. In doing this, I relate to the "Cowboy Way" to express my thoughts and feelings. I am a simple man. I put my pants on the same as all of you, one leg at a time. In this book, you will not see many big and fancy words. I like simple and easy to understand things. That is how the Lord's word is – Plain and Simple.

My goal is to reach people out there that are lost souls, not knowing where to turn. I will be sharing my story in this book on how I came to know the Lord and how my walk got started, along with all the blessings He has given my family and me.

What's Your Story?

1 Peter 3:15 (NIV)
But in your hearts set apart CHRIST as LORD. Always be prepared to give an answer to everyone who asks you to give the reason for the hope that you have. But do this with gentleness and respect.

Sharing one's story about their life and how they came to know the Lord is important. Each of us has a story to tell. In telling your story to others, we can relate and help each other out on our walk. For the first twenty-one years of my life, I never stepped into a church but a few times, and yet I did not know why I was there. Church and God were not my thing back then. Hanging out with my friends, drinking, chasing the girls, and working was all I thought about. Little did I know the plans that God had for me later in life.

Proverbs 16:9
In his heart a man plans his course,
but the Lord determines his steps. (NIV)

After graduating from High School in 1977, I started working for my dad, Bill. A man whom I respect and love very much. A man who taught me about life and how to work hard. We worked on the oil rigs together, and he was tough on me. At times, I hated him for it. It was not until later in life I realized how much he was teaching me about life in general.

Psalm 90:12
Teach us to realize the brevity of life,
so that we may grow in wisdom. (ESV)

We ended up in Rangely, Colorado with our rig. Our Company man was Newt Burkhalter, whom later would turn out to be my Father-In-Law. Got to tell you, I feared this man, he was intimidating. There was something about him, though, that I liked… he had a heart of gold, was caring, and a man of God who would stand up for right and wrong. Later, Newt talked my dad and me into going to Cisco, Utah, 50 miles west of Grand Junction, Colorado, to work over some oil wells. We agreed to workover a few oil and gas wells but ended up doing even more work and decided on moving to Grand Junction. Newt moved his family from Glenwood Springs, Colorado to Grand Junction as well. I had met Newt's family and did not even realize before that he had four beautiful daughters and his wife, Sue. Now, Sue, I cannot say enough about her, she was a very caring and spiritual lady who over the years, became like a mother to me.

Mathew 25:34-36

Then the King will say to those on his right, "Come, you who are blessed by my Father; take your inheritance, the kingdom prepared for you since the creation of the world. For I was hungry, and you gave me something to eat, I was thirsty, and you gave me something to drink. I was a stranger, and you invited me in, I needed clothes, and you clothed me, I was sick, and you looked after me. I was in prison, and you came to visit me." (NIV)

I remember a little the first time I went to church with Newt and his family: at that time, I was dating his daughter, Kim. Sue would tell me she remembered that day like it was yesterday. She said I was sitting in the car in the parking lot of the church and sweat was pouring down my face. To be honest, I think I would have rather gone out and fought a grizzly bear than to walk into that church. I was scared. After service, I thought to myself "It wasn't that bad!" The people were nice and polite, I am not sure what the preacher talked about, but I was not going to let my guard down until I really checked this God thing out. Newt told me later that he mentioned to Sue, that the first time he met me, the Holy Spirit was telling him to take me under his wing. Looking back, I can see where God was with me in my life and journey. I just did not realize it at the time because I would not let Him into my life back then.

Pushing cows up Sheep Creek

Newt on Ole Gus

Joshua 1:9

Have I not commanded you? Be strong and courageous. Do not be terrified; do not be discouraged, for the LORD your God will be with you wherever you go. (ESU)

The year was 1980. On May 17th I married the love of my life Kimberly Sue. You will also see me mention her as Kim or Kimmy. Together, we raised four beautiful children, two boys and two girls. Now back to the God thing and having my guard up. Of course, I kept going to church with Kim and the kids, and I was getting some valuable information from the Ole Preacher but during all that time going to church, I just could not connect to this God thing. I do not think I was ready to turn myself over completely. The one thing I really respected about Sue and Newt is they never shoved it onto me. I know they prayed for me all the time. Between God, Sue, and Newt, the foundation was building slowly. I relate my story to me being a wild mustang and Kimmy roping me and working with me slow (Teaching me Gods word) and occasionally she would pull me in with that rope. I would come in cautious, sometimes not liking what I saw, I would turn and run but Kim never let go of that rope no matter what. And I thank her sincerely for always being there when I needed her.

Psalm 81:11-12
But my people would not listen to Me; Israel would not submit to Me. So I gave them over to their stubborn hearts to follow their own devices. (NIV)

God sometimes lets us continue in our stubbornness to bring us to our senses. He does not keep us from rebelling because He wants us to learn the consequences of our sins. He uses these experiences to turn people away from greater sin and to have faith in Him.

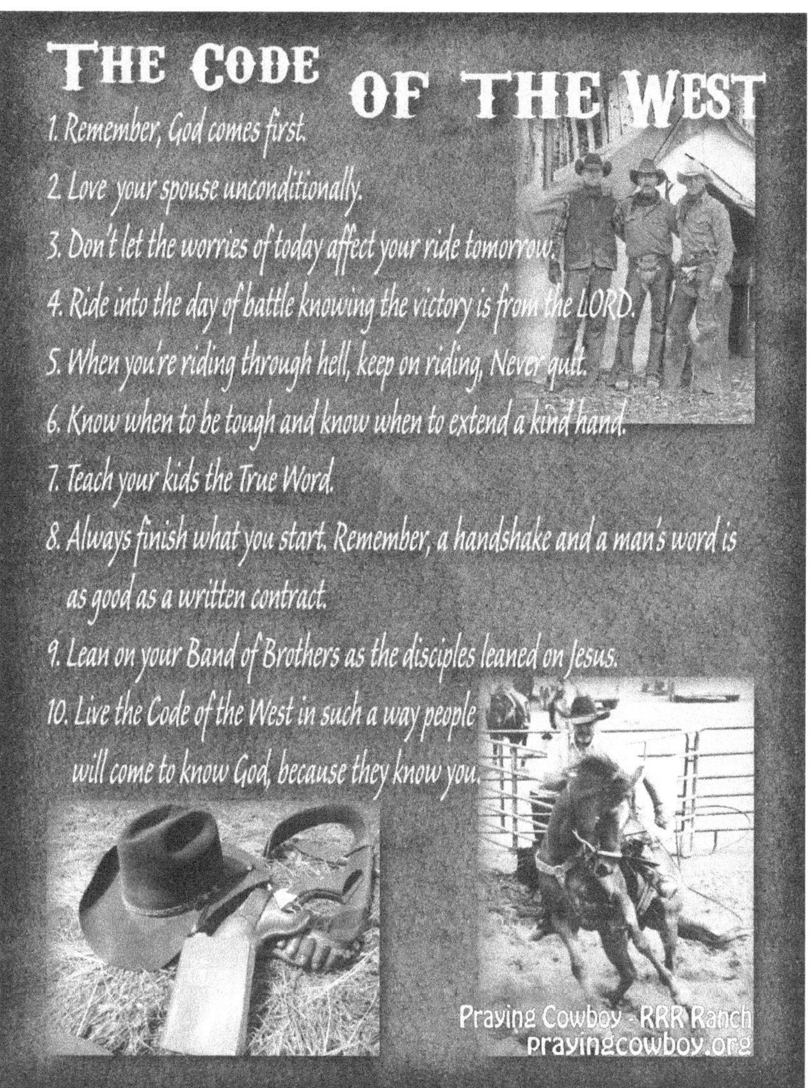
THE CODE OF THE WEST
1. Remember, God comes first.
2. Love your spouse unconditionally.
3. Don't let the worries of today affect your ride tomorrow.
4. Ride into the day of battle knowing the victory is from the LORD.
5. When you're riding through hell, keep on riding, Never quit.
6. Know when to be tough and know when to extend a kind hand.
7. Teach your kids the True Word.
8. Always finish what you start. Remember, a handshake and a man's word is as good as a written contract.
9. Lean on your Band of Brothers as the disciples leaned on Jesus.
10. Live the Code of the West in such a way people will come to know God, because they know you.
Praying Cowboy - RRR Ranch
prayingcowboy.org

Remember, God Comes First

Matthew 22:37,38 (NIV)
Jesus replied; "Love the Lord your God with all your heart and with all your soul and with all your mind."
This is the first and greatest commandment.

Back in the Old West Days, when Cowboys and settlers roamed the earth, it was a lot different than it is today. Back then, men, women, and children did not have much to their name. Most cowboys had what they owned in their saddlebags behind their horse with their bedroll. In those saddlebags, some cowboys carried what they called the "Good Book." (The Bible) Cowboys talk about "The Man Upstairs" and often you hear the phrase "God and Jesus." It was a tough life back then but a good one. Cowboys were loners, and most of them didn't have anyone to turn to, comfort them, or love them, even when they were in trouble. They were on their own. Most of them knew the Man upstairs would take care of them, comfort them and love them in their desire of need. Cowboys put God first in their lives. One of my favorite movies ~ Lonesome Dove. It's about pushing thousands of cows from Texas to Montana. It took a lot of hard work and determination.

It was a dream that Gus and McCall had. They wanted to see Montana before they were too old. Sounds like fun, right? This is nothing like the movie, City Slickers. Back in the old days, cowboys would be in the saddle fourteen hours a day, and cows strung out for several miles with "greenhorns" at the tail end picking up the strays and eating dust. Most times, they would do 10 miles a day. A tough life but a good life. Of course, working seven days a week with no days off, cowboys "church" was being out in God's Creation.

What cowboys had to face on their daily journey could cost them their lives, facing ruthless Indians, stampede's, disease, or their horse going down on them. Cowboys had a lot of hardships to deal with out on the open range in Gods' creation. The one thing they had, that we are all subject to, is our Father above and relying on Him to take care of us in tough times by putting Him first in our lives.

Proverbs 3:6
'In all your ways acknowledge Him,
and he will make your paths straight." (NIV)

To receive God's guidance, said Solomon, we must acknowledge God in all our ways. This means turning every area of our life over to Him. Look at your values and priorities. What is important to you? What is His advicc? In many arcas of your lifc, you may already acknowledge God, but it is in the areas where you try to restrict or ignore His influence that will cause you grief. Make Him a vital part of everything you do. Then He will guide you because you will be worthy of doing His purpose.

In today's world, we are at such a fast pace, demanding time from our lives right now. Satan comes in the middle of the night as the prowling lion to destroy and kill.

Job 1:12
The Lord said to Satan, "Very well, then, everything he has is in your hands, but on the man himself do not lay a finger." Then Satan went out from the presence of the Lord. (NIV)

If you were asked, "What or who comes first in your life?" Of course, most of you would say "God comes first in my life." That is easy to say, but do we really mean it? Let's say, Jesus was walking on earth right now in human form and He comes to your house and says to you. "Sell everything you have, give it all to the needy, and follow Me to spread the good word and make me disciples of the world." "Whoa, whoa, Lord, do you see everything I have, a beautiful mansion, lots of money. I have worked hard for all this, and you expect me to just give it all away?"

John 3:16
"For God so loved the world that He gave His one and only Son, that whoever believes in Him shall not perish but have eternal life." (NIV)

In this life on earth, we all have two choices, Heaven or Hell. The first choice is what we all should want. Back before my walk got strong with God, I was not putting Him first in my life. I had other priorities I thought were more important, back then, God was down in my priority list, which I will share more of later.

Love Your Spouse Unconditionally

Proverbs 31:10
"The wife of noble character who can find? She is worth far more than rubies." (NIV)

Now men, I know spouse means a man or woman, but what I really want to emphasize on is our beauty, partner in life, best friend, mother of our children, someone to comfort us in challenging times and to love us unconditionally.

Proverbs 31:12
She brings him good, not harm, all the days of her life." (NIV)

That, gentlemen, is our wives. This is an important topic that needs to be discussed. I work at this every day and still fall short of my goals in loving my wife as Christ loved the church.

Ephesians 5:25-27
Husbands, love your wives, just as Christ loved the church and gave Himself up for her to make her holy, cleansing her by the washing with water through the word, and to present her to Himself as a radiant church, without stain or wrinkle or any other blemish, but holy and blameless. (NIV)

God gave us men a partner to love, bear us children, comfort us, watch over our household affairs, and support us men in everything we do. A woman's job is never done. We, us men, could never and will never be able to do the job of a woman.

Proverbs 31:10-31

A wife of noble character who can find? She is worth far more than rubies. Her husband has full confidence in her and lacks nothing of value. She brings him good, not harm, all the days of her life. She selects wool and flax and works with eager hands. She is like the merchant ships, bringing her food from afar. She gets up while it is still dark; she provides food for her family and portions for her servant girls. She considers a field and buys it; out of her earnings she plants a vineyard. She sets about her work vigorously; her arms are strong for the task. She sees that her trading is profitable, and her lamp does not go out at night. In her hand she holds the distaff and grasps the spindle with her fingers. She opens her arms to the poor and extends her hands to the needy. When it snows, she has no fear for her household; for all of them are clothed in scarlet. She makes coverings for her bed; she is clothed in fine linen and purple. Her husband is respected at the city gate, where he takes his seat among the elders of the land. She makes linen garments and sells them and supplies the merchants with sashes. She is clothed with strength and dignity; she can laugh at the days to come. She speaks with wisdom, and faithful instruction is on her tongue. She watches over the affairs of her household and does not eat the bread of idleness. Her children arise and call her blessed; her husband also, and he praises her; Many women do noble things, but you surpass them all. Charm is deceptive, and beauty is fleeting; but a woman who fears the LORD is to be praised. Give her the reward she has earned, and let her works bring her praise at the city gate. (NIV)

Proverbs has a lot to say about the woman. How fitting that the book ends with a picture of a woman of strong character, great wisdom, many skills, and great compassion. Some people have the mistaken idea that the ideal woman in the bible is retiring, a servile and entirely domestic. Not so! This woman is an excellent wife and mother. She is also the manufacturer, upholsterer, manager, realtor, farmer, seamstress, importer and merchant. Her strength and dignity do not come from her amazing achievements, however. They are a result of her reverence for God.

In our society, where physical appearance counts for so much, it surprises us to realize her appearance is never mentioned. Her attractiveness comes entirely from her character. The woman described in this chapter has outstanding abilities. Her family's social position is high. In fact, she may not be one woman at all, she may be a composition portrait of ideal womanhood. Do not use her as a model to imitate in every detail; your days are not long enough to do everything she does! See her instead as an inspiration to be all you can be. We cannot be just like her, but we can learn from her industry, integrity, and resourcefulness.

The cowboys back in the old days treated women with such respect, just like the cowboys today. They all had a Code of The West to live by. Some people might ask, "Were these rules written down?" No, they lived by them. Every cowboy knew these rules, right from wrong. And of course, some ruthless cowboys did not follow these rules, but they would pay the price. Women back then had a rough life and were respected for their courage and hard work. Cowboys would respect a lady with the tip of their hats, saying "*Ma'am, or Miss.*" When walking with a lady, he would be arm in arm and would never walk ahead of her. If a cowboy ever slapped a lady in public or even in private, he would pay the ultimate price and pray that he would have never done that after getting the beating of his life. Cowboys would risk their lives to protect their women. A friend of mine was telling me about a conference meeting he was having with employees, and during this meeting he asked this question to eight men. "How many of you would take a bullet for your wife?" They all sat there and had to think about it for a while and a few of them said they "might" take a bullet for their wife depending on the circumstances. The others said, "Definitely not." Now I know that is only eight men, a small percent. If you were asked the same question, what would your answer be? I know what my answer is without even thinking twice about it. I would die for my wife. I am her Warrior, to love, cherish, and protect her no matter what the price.

Genesis 2:21-24

So the LORD GOD caused the man to fall into a deep sleep; and while he was sleeping, He took one of the man's ribs and closed up the place with flesh. Then the LORD GOD made a woman from the rib He had taken out of the man, He brought her to the man. The man said, "This is now bone of my bones and flesh of my flesh; she shall be called woman, for she was taken out of man." For this reason, a man will leave his father and mother and be united to his wife, and they become one flesh. (NIV)

My wife and I were married in 1980. Thirty-seven years together when I started drafting this book. Now I *wish* I could sit here and tell you all that we have had a perfect marriage, but I would be lying. We have had our tough times with each other, and looking back on my life, God was not a part of *my* marriage. Now my wife Kim, God was big with her in our marriage. I would rarely pray with her and would not read the bible much with her. Now, with my walk being stronger with the Lord, young couples will ask me, "what's your advice on marriage?" I don't tell them it will not work; I tell them that if both of you do not have God strong in your lives and your marriage, it will be tough.

Song of Songs 5:16

His mouth is sweetness itself; he is altogether lovely. This is my lover, this my friend, O daughters of Jerusalem. (NIV)

Quite a few years ago, at a hunting camp, up in Gods' beautiful creation, I was getting some pack horses loaded up with gear. I was taking my preacher, Chris, into our Spike campsite, 9000' into the wilderness country, to spend some time archery hunting. While we were getting ready, Chris was talking about all the different countries he and his wife had been through in the world. After listening to him for a while, I looked at him and said, "Yeah, Chris, all my wife has ever talked about is how much she dreams of going to Hawaii on vacation." And I said to her," Honey, why would I want to go to Hawaii, I've never left anything there." Chris walked over to me, the look on his face, I was thinking to myself, *what did I say wrong?* Well, he unloaded on me while tapping me on the chest, telling me how the cow ate the cabbage. *"Let me tell you something, brother, our wives support us men in everything we do, whether its hunting, fishing with our friends, golfing, going to a football game, or going wherever we men decide on. They support us a hundred percent of the time, but in turn, when they want to do something or go somewhere of their choice, we have a tough time supporting them."* I stood there just looking at him for a moment, he really hit me hard on what he just said. I know it was God talking to me through him. That was in September. After Chris said that to me, for months it lingered on my mind. Our wives are the ones that organize these vacations we go on, getting airline tickets, reservations for the trip at motels, and different things that take a lot of preparation and time, which us men do not have time to do. To be honest, most of us men do not have the ability. The New Year came around and it was January. Now men, I took my wife to Hawaii! I was so proud of myself. I planned this trip for her and me, and she never had any idea. It was tough, but I got it done. Many hours on the phone making all the arrangements (I had help from her sweet sister, Heather) having enough points on our credit card to fly us both round trip for free and saving enough petty cash for expenses. It was an amazing trip, and I thank God for that special day with the preacher at hunting camp, where my eyes were opened. When your wife asks you to go somewhere or someplace with her, like going to the movies, and the first thing you ask is, "What is the movie about? Oh, a love story, why don't you go with your sister or mom?" Or they may ask, "Will you go to my friend's wedding with me?"" Honey, I do not know anyone there, and they are boring, NO!" Or she will ask the big question, "Honey, will you go to church with me, please?" And you reply, "Maybe next week, I am busy today." Men, brothers, we must open our eyes up to our beauty, or one day our beauty won't be there. Our wives love us men, because they cherish us, and we are their heroes and warriors.

Don't Let The Worries Of Today Affect Your Ride Tomorrow

Matthew 6:25-27

"Therefore I tell you, do not worry about your life, what you will eat or drink; or about your body, what you will wear. Is not life more important than food, and the body more important than clothes? Look at the birds of the air; they do not sow or reap or stow away in barns, and yet your Heavenly Father feeds them. Are you not much more valuable than they? Who of you by worrying can add a single hour to his life?" (NIV)

Worry may (1) Damage your health. (2) Cause the object of your worry to consume your thoughts. (3) Disrupt your productivity. (4) Negatively affect the way you treat others, and (5) Reduce your ability to trust in God. The difference between worry and genuine concern – worry immobilizes, but concern moves you to action.

SEVEN REASONS NOT TO WORRY (NIV)

6:25 – The same God who created life in you can be trusted with the details of your life.

6:26 – Worrying about the future hampers your efforts for today.

6:27 – Worrying Is more harmful than helpful.

6:28-30 – God does not ignore those who depend on Him.

6:31,32 – Worrying shows a lack of faith in understanding of God.

6:33 – There are challenges God wants us to pursue, and worrying keeps us from them.

6:34 – Living one day at a time keeps us from being consumed with worry.

Worrying can be harmful to your health, your body, your attitude, and harmful to your marriage. When there is so much worrying, it can affect our daily lives. As humans, it is natural to take these worries on ourselves and try to solve them on our own. I know that even with my walk as strong as it is, I still catch myself trying to solve problems allowing them to consume me with worry, never getting anything done all day. Then, I look up and it is like I see God smiling at me saying, "Give it to me son, all you must do is ask, that is what I am here for." Satan is exceptionally good at his scheme to consume us with worry and not to do the Lord's work. None of us can see into the future to predict what is in store for us. We need to concentrate on today because tomorrow may not be here. We need to have strong faith that God will see us through our everyday situations throughout our journey.

Philippians 4:6-7

Do not be anxious about anything, but in everything, by prayer and petition, with thanksgiving, present your request to God. And the peace of God, which transcends all understanding, will guard your hearts and your minds in Jesus Christ. (NIV)

Imagine never being 'anxious about anything'!

It seems like an impossibility – we all have worries on the job, in our homes, and at school. But Paul's advice is to turn our worries into prayers. Do you want to worry less? Then pray more! Whenever you start to feel worried, stop and pray.

More Of My Story: God Is Always In Control Of Our Lives

Back in my younger days, just after getting married, and starting a family, life was great. I was working a lot in the oilfields and making a good living, always having food on the table and a roof over our heads. I vowed to have Kim stay at home to raise the kids the right way, take care of the household, and of course, watch over me, guiding me in the way of the Lord. She had a big task on her hands to bring me closer to the Lord. Back in 2007, I was visiting with Chris, who used to be our preacher at N.E. Christian Church. We were talking away about the old days when Chris started chuckling and said, "I remember to this day when I came to your house, and we visited about God for the first time together." Chris told me I sat at my desk, arms crossed, wearing my muscle T-shirt with my feet propped up, cowboy boots on, looking tough. Right then, Chris knew he had his work cut out for me. I know Chris did a lot of praying for me. He was a good mentor. One of the things I really respect him for was he never shoved this God thing onto me either. He did build the foundation of God with the help of Kim, Newt, and Sue. When it came time for praying, well that was not my thing. I remember listening to preachers, and other Christians pray. I thought, "Whoa those people are awesome, they are professionals." All the big words they used! Some I did not even know the definition of. I told myself there was no way I could hold a candle to these people, telling myself, "No praying in public." Later in my walk, I realized, God doesn't care about the big words, He wants our prayers to come from the heart with sincerity.

Psalm 4:3

Know that the Lord has set apart the godly for Himself; The Lord will hear when I call to Him. (NIV)

Back in the '90's, my Father-in-law, Brother-in-law Sean, my son Chase and I flew to Atlanta, Georgia to attend a Promise Keepers Convention, where thousands of men were also attending. We walked into this big convention and Chase, and I were the only two with cowboy hats on. Not that this convention has anything to do with what is on top of our heads, but we were asked a lot if we were real cowboys. I told Chase, "I don't think they see to many cowboys in the city." When the big event started, somehow, the four of us were picked by the staff along with several others to volunteer our time as prayer warriors, so when intermission came, we had to stand out in the hallways and pray with anyone who needed prayer. Of course, they stuck these tags on us, so the men knew who to come to for prayer – my stomach was in knots. I told Sean that I do not remember signing up for this part and that I had never prayed for a stranger. So, what I did, which was bad, I would be standing there watching these men and when I would see one making a b-line towards me, I would give the dirtiest, meanest look until they would turn and look for someone else. I can take a guess as to what you are thinking right now, you are either laughing or thinking "what a jerk." I was.

When we had big family dinners, of course, the head of the household had to say the blessing before the meal. I got out of that one too. Before dinner was served, I would corner Kimmy and tell her, "Honey, please have your dad say the blessing." She would give me a look and say, "Chicken!" I was then, I didn't know the importance of prayer. Kim was a tremendous help on the praying subject, really being patient with me, knowing I would come around one day.

Ride Into The Day Of Battle Knowing Victory Is From Lord

Job 39:19-25

Do you give the horse his strength or clothe his neck with a flowing mane? Do you make him leap like a locust, striking terror with his proud snorting? He paws fiercely, rejoicing in his strength, and charges into the fray. He laughs at fear, afraid of

nothing; he does not shy away from the sword. The quiver rattles against his side, along with the flashing spear and lance. In frenzied excitement he eats up the ground; he cannot stand still when the trumpet sounds. At the blast of the trumpet he snorts, "Aha!" He catches the scent of the battle from afar, the shout of commanders and the battle cry. (NIV)

Most of us are riding into battle every day, whether it be at work, at school, an illness, or family issues. These are battles we face every day in our lives that we cannot fight on our own. We need help, we need the Lord leading and guiding us, giving us the wisdom to help us win. At the end of the battles, the glory and the victory go to the Lord.

The movie Secretariat (one of my all-time favorite movies) is about a lady named Penny Chenery, who is faced with a choice, after her mother passed on and her father is in poor health, of selling Claiborne Farm, her family's horse racing farm. The farm was in a bad financial situation, Penny must decide to take the straightforward way out and sell or keep it and fight the battle of her life. She made the right choice. She chose to stay and fight the battle knowing the victory would come from the Lord. This is a true and inspiring story. The movie has clear invocation of Gods will throughout it and many positive references to Jesus in the songs that energize and support the inspirational victories. It also has an opening quote from the book of Job that becomes the major theme. Furthermore, there are actions that acknowledge a Christian worldview, God's' victory, and His magnificent creations, as represented by the amazing title character, Secretariat. The film upholds such biblical and moral values such as honoring your parents and doing the right thing. After Secretariat won the Preakness, Pimlico general manager Chick Long said, "It is as if God decided to create the perfect horse." 'Secretariat' can be summed up in one verse.

2 Timothy 4:7
I have fought the good fight, I have finished the race, I have kept the faith. (NIV)

You know, as Christians, we are in a battle every day of our lives, fighting the evil and corruption of this world today. Satan is the prince of this world, but if we fight our battles with the Lord's help, God is going to be victorious through us. I have been in a lot of battles during my life, and back in my younger years, I thought I was fighting them on my own. As I look back now, I realize I was not by myself fighting them, God was there every step of the way. I give Him glory and victory. I thank him for that and praise Him.

The next time you are facing a battle in your life, do not lay down and quit. Take the time to go into prayer and ask God to help you and give you the wisdom and courage to fight your battle, always giving God the glory and victory, He deserves.

When You're Going Through Hell, Keep On Riding. Never quit.

This is one of my favorite sayings that I tell people a lot. I strived to bring my kids up this way as that was the way my dad brought me up. Never quit, no matter how tough it gets out there. Of course, there have been several times that I figured quitting would have been so much easier. Something inside of me just would not allow that. That was the little voice in my head saying, "Don't quit, you will get through this." Back then, I did not know it was the Holy Spirit talking to me. When you want to give up, you are missing what God has to offer.

2 Chronicles 15:7
"But as for you, be strong and do not give up,
for your work will be rewarded." (NIV)

God put such a magnificent creature on this earth called a horse. One of the brothers once told me that the horse is mentioned more in the bible than any other animal. I haven't checked that part out for myself, but this brother knows his bible well. Other than the horse, God has blessed us humans with many different animals and pets to give us comfort and love us. When you come home from an exhausting day and turn into your driveway, here comes your dog running and wagging his tail, so happy to see you. Don't tell me that after having a difficult day, when you see your dog happily running to you, it doesn't brighten your day. God put pets on this earth not only for our enjoyment, but to also take care of them. The point I am trying to make here is that these animals can teach us a lot about life and about ourselves if we just learn to listen to them. Of course, I know animals can't talk and they don't have to for us to learn. If we pay attention and watch them, they are speaking to us through their actions. God is so amazing to have put such creatures on this earth to give us enjoyment and companionship.

Luke 22:43-44
An angel from Heaven appeared to Him and strengthened Him. And being in anguish, He prayed more earnestly, and His sweat was like drops of blood falling to the ground. (NIV)

Jesus was in extreme agony, but He did not give up or give in. He went ahead with the mission for which He had come.

Quite a few years ago at hunting camp, up in the Muddy Wilderness above Paonia, Colorado, me and several of our hunting friends had an episode of what it was like riding through hell. Our horses taught us a valuable lesson about never quitting no matter how tough it gets and how tough it can get in life.

Psalm 19:1-6

THE HEAVENS DECLARE THE GLORY OF GOD; AND THE FIRMAMENT SHEWETH HIS HANDYWORK. DAY UNTO DAY UTTERETH SPEECH, AND NIGHT UNTO NIGHT SHEWETH KNOWLEDGE. THERE IS NO SPEECH NOR LANGUAGE WHERE THEIR VOICE IS NOT HEARD. THEIR LINE IS GONE OUT THROUGH ALL THE EARTH, AND THEIR WORDS TO THE END OF THE WORLD. IN THEM HATH HE SET A TABERNACLE FOR THE SUN, WHICH IS AS A BRIDEGROOM COMING OUT OF HIS CHAMBER, AND REJOICETH AS A STRONG MAN TO RUN A RACE. HIS GOING FORTH IS FROM THE END OF THE HEAVEN, AND HIS CIRCUIT UNTO THE ENDS OF IT: AND THERE IS NOTHING HID FROM THE HEAT THEREOF. (KJV)

We were hunting one afternoon, probably an hour or better from Spike Camp, up a big valley around 8500'. Such beautiful country, it is hard to describe how beautiful God's creation is, that is where I feel closest to Him. I heard a saying once, "I would rather be in God's country thinking about Him than to be sitting in a church thinking about being out in God's country."

While hunting, most of the day, a storm settled in on us, and the cloud coverage got so low you couldn't see 50 feet in front of you. Late that afternoon, we all met back where the horses were tied up. My boys and I were hunting with our Texas friends, Larry, and his son Robbie. Larry, Robbie, and their families are close to ours. We had met Larry over 20 years ago hunting up Leon Creek above Vega Reservoir. When we met, Larry and his group of Texans had been camping a few hundred yards away from us. One night they invited Newt and me over for a sit-down dinner around the campfire. A great bunch of guys, the kind that would give you the shirt off their backs and drop whatever they were doing to help you out, if needed. One thing about Texans is they are good cooks. We would meet every year at hunting camp. Back then, I did not have many close friends, but God changed that for my family and me on the friendship with Larry and his family. After a few years hunting at Leon Creek, we decided to move on. Lots of hunters, 4-wheelers, motorcycles and motor homes contributed to pushing all the game out. We ended up leaving Leon Creek and found The Muddy, which is northwest of the Majestic Ragged Mountains above Paonia, Colorado. We invited Larry and his bunch to come with us. There was just something about these Texans and their friendship that I did not want to lose.

Proverbs 18:24

"A man of many companions may come to ruin, but there is a friend who sticks closer than a brother." (NIV)

Loneliness is everywhere – many people feel cut off and alienated from others. We all need friends who stick close, listen, care, and offer help when it is needed – in good times and bad. It is better to have one such friend than dozens of superficial acquaintances.

Larry had met Newt and Wendell (Newt's Dad), and my two boys up at Leon Creek. The one thing Larry was amazed about was how young my boys were, eight and nine years old, going up to hunting camp and sleeping in an old sheep herder's tent. We had met Larry's son Robbie later in the years at the Muddy. Robbie was a gentleman, just an awesome young man. He became a close and dear friend to my sons and the rest of the family.

Larry was always trying to get our family to Texas to go hunting on their ranch for whitetail, pigs, and a few rattlesnakes here and there. It took about ten years for him to convince us to go out there and meet the rest of his family. Larry's wife Linda is amazing. The love she has in her heart and the way she cares for others is remarkable. Larry was always bragging like Texans do about his Texas mountains on the ranch. When I saw his so called mountains, I looked at him and said, "Larry, we call those ant hills in Colorado." I think it hurt his feelings because he looked at me and replied, "You're in Texas now, that's our mountains."" Okay Larry, okay." That was a trip I will never forget, a priceless time with family and friends and of course we bagged plenty of game down there. When Larry and I first met, God was never mentioned between us. It was not until years down the road when he and Robbie joined us on another hunting trip (I had just begun my walk with the Lord) that they mentioned they could see a tremendous change in me and thought it was incredible. I gave them a (NIV) Cowboy Bible, prayed before each meal, and again prayed before we went riding. They were both shocked at how my walk with the Lord had changed me. It is amazing once you finally realize that you cannot do the things in life on your own. Each of us has a time and place when we finally let the Lord into our hearts and give Him the reins to guide us.

Psalm 25:4-5

"SHOW ME YOUR WAYS, O LORD; TEACH ME YOUR PATHS; GUIDE ME IN YOUR TRUTH AND TEACH ME, FOR YOU ARE GOD MY SAVIOR, AND MY HOPE IS IN YOU ALL DAY LONG." (NIV)

Listening to God is like listening to your horse. God will lead you down the straight and narrow path, protect you from the pitfalls and dangers that can get in your way. Back to the story of the ride through Hell. We were one canyon over from our main camp up the Little Muddy at the base of Spruce Mountain. As the crow flies, we were not too far away from what we called East Canyon. However, riding time was about an hour and a half of tough country and down timber, but the elk hunting was great. The boys and I tend to go into the roughest, toughest places where no one else will go because that is where the elk are. We always told the boys, "Do not ever tell your mom or grandma the rough places we take you, or they will never let you come back hunting with us!" With a smile they vowed, "Don't worry dad and Grandpa we won't say a word." I did not know at the time, but Grandpa Newt and I were building and teaching our boys how to be warriors – God's Warriors for Him. What a blessing my two sons have been to Kim and myself throughout our everyday lives.

1 Chronicles 12:1-2
THESE WERE THE MEN WHO CAME TO DAVID AT ZIKLAG, WHILE HE WAS BANISHED FROM THE PRESENCE OF SAUL SON OF KISH (THEY WERE AMONG THE WARRIORS WHO HELPED HIM IN BATTLE THEY WERE ARMED WITH BOWS AND WERE ABLE TO SHOOT ARROWS OR TO SLING STONES RIGHT-HANDED OR LEFT-HANDED; THEY WERE KINSMEN OF SAUL FROM THE TRIBE OF BENJAMIN): (NIV)

We all met back at the horses in East Canyon, checking cinches and placing our gear back on the saddles and getting ready to head back to camp, and none of us realizing the ride through Hell was about to happen. My boys Luke and Chase, Larry, and his son Robbie were all ready to mount. Low clouds hung just above us, and suddenly it was like the gates of Hell opened. Down through the canyons came wind like I had never seen before, snow, sleet and rain, thunder, and lightning (yes, lightning in a snowstorm) racing throughout the clouds. In all my years of hunting and riding, I had never been in something like this. I have always told the boys to always be ready, the weather can change in five minutes from sunny to bad and if you are not prepared with the right clothing and gear, you might not survive. I never worried much about my sons and daughters in severe weather because I taught them how to survive when things got tough in all aspects of life. Never to quit, God is always at your side leading you the right way, and to never lose your faith in Him. While Larry was sitting on his horse and the fierce wind going right through our wool clothing, I walked over to make sure everything was good. He looked down and asked, “Have you ever been in this kind of weather before?” I looked back up at him with that ole cowboy grin and said, “Nope, but don’t worry Larry the horses will get us back to camp with God leading the way.” We were all worried about the wind and lightning in the clouds, not knowing if this might be our time to go with the Lord. My biggest concern was how hard the wind was howling and that a tree might come down on top of us and our horses. With the wind so fierce and the snow and the sleet pounding at us, we had to keep our heads down to battle the situation. Even the horses had their heads low to the ground fighting inch by inch through the weather to get us back to camp safely. After several hours and what seemed like an eternity of struggling to stay on the course, our horses all stopped at once. Not knowing for sure where we were, we looked up and we all realized the horses had us back at camp. Still fighting the wind and snow, the care for the horses came first. We unsaddled and fed them before we went to the comforts of building a fire to get warm ourselves. All our jackets were froze solid, we had to get some warmth in them before we could take them off. While sitting by the fire with some hot coffee in our cups, along with a few shots of Jack Daniels, we all knew the ride we just rode was through Hell. With all the circumstances out there, we never quit trying, with God guiding our horses to camp, an adventure I will never forget. A lesson our horses taught us in courage, trust and to never quit no matter how tough it gets.

As some of you go through your own Hell, even now as I draft this book, I fear some of you will not tough it out and you will quit. God hates when you quit, He has a plan for each one of us. He is not going to make it easy. But if we stick it out, the rewards at the end will be great. If you quit on your journey that God has laid out in front of you, you will never find happiness in your life.

Galatians 6:9
LET US NOT BECOME WEARY IN DOING GOOD, FOR AT THE PROPER TIME WE WILL REAP A HARVEST IF WE DO NOT GIVE UP. (NIV)

Know When To Be Tough And When To Extend A Kind Hand

JAMES 2:1-10

"My, Brothers, show no partiality as you hold the faith in our Lord Jesus Christ, the Lord of glory. For if a man wearing a gold ring and fine clothing comes into your assembly, and a poor man in shabby clothing also comes in, and if you pay attention to the one who wears the fine clothing say, "You sit here in a good place," while you say to the poor man "You stand over there," or "sit down at my feet," have you not then made distinctions amongst yourselves and become judges with evil thoughts? Listen, my beloved brothers, has not God chosen those who are poor in the world to be rich in faith and heirs of the kingdom, which He has promised to those who love Him? But you have dishonored the poor man. Are not the rich ones who oppress you, and the ones who drag you into court? Are they not the ones who blaspheme the honorable name by which you were called? If you really fulfill the royal law according to the Scripture, "You shall love your neighbor as yourself," you are doing well. But if you show partiality, you are committing sin and are convicted by the law as transgressors. For whoever keeps the whole law but fails in one point has become guilty of all of it." (NIV)

This is a tough and cruel world that we live in today. As Christians, we must be tough when the time comes, and we need to know when to extend a kind hand. The Non-Christians think that we Christians are not tough and that we are supposed to always be nice, no matter the circumstances. More or less, us Christians are wimps in their eyes. That is what I believed back before my walk started, and how wrong I was. There are a lot of Christians (out there) that when the tough times come, they can be tough. The Bible gives examples on how God's people and disciples were tough when they needed to be, but they also knew when they needed to extend a kind hand. In the New Testament, I read where Jesus entered the Temple area and drove out all who were buying and selling there. He overturned the tables of the money changers and the benches of those selling doves. "It is written," He said to them, "My house will be called a house of prayer, but you are making it a den of robbers." The blind and the lame came to Him at the temple, and He healed them. Going back to the verses of James 2:1-10; these are incredibly great verses that I can relate to during an episode that happened to me over twenty years ago. I was involved with a group that sold all kinds of merchandise. It was a pyramid scheme where you brought on distributors below you to order products, and you would make a percentage of profit off their purchases. I know many others are familiar with these types of sales gimmicks.

We had several meetings where we would invite others who wanted a better lifestyle to free themselves financially. There was one meeting where there were going to be a large amount of people coming and the man who would be speaking was exceedingly high up in the organization. I was running late, working on the oil rigs and did not have time to clean up before the meeting. Of course, I was in shabby, dirty clothing not looking pretty, but I felt it was important to be there and support the guest speaker. The presentation went well, and afterwards some of us went to a coffee shop. After a while, I got up to leave, having to work early the next morning and as I was leaving, I wanted to thank the gentleman who did the presentation and let him know I appreciated him, his time and for traveling such a great distance to be here. Walking over, he was visiting with two young couples in a booth with his back to me. As I approached the table and tapped him on the shoulder, he turned, looked at me and then turned right back around, continuing his conversation with the others at his table and told them, "Now you can get into this organization and gain financial freedom, or you can be like this man (me) and spend the rest of your life working hard labor and never getting anywhere in life." He did not acknowledge me or that I was still standing there. As I turned around and walked out the door, I left the group and never returned. While I was driving home, I felt hurt, and I was mad. I had known this gentleman for quite some time and could not believe what he said to the other people around him about me, while knowing I was right there. I was embarrassed. I learned an important lesson that day, I learned not to judge on the way anyone is dressed. I also learned when to be tough or to be kind, but most importantly if the battle was worth my energy. It wasn't this man had already shown he was just there to belittle me and others. It was tougher to walk away than to say something. I forgave this man for embarrassing me and I appreciated the lesson I learned I learned from him.

Back in the old days of the cowboy era, Cowboys were rough and tough and had lots of determination to get their job done. When a cowboy hired onto an outfit, he rode for that brand. Once he threw his bedroll into the wagon, there was no quitting along the way. He finished the job no matter how tough it got. The ranch foreman was tough in a way that would gain the cowboys respect and the foreman hated quitters. A good foreman knew when it was time to extend a kind hand to help another in need, and he knew it was his responsibility. When he told a cowboy, "Good job" that was one of the greatest accomplishments they would hear from their boss.

Colossians 3:12
"Therefore, as God's chosen people, holy and dearly loved, clothe yourselves with compassion, kindness, humility, gentleness and patience." (NIV)

Today's society and work force have changed dramatically. If the boss is tough on an employee, the boss gets written up, or even fired. Over the years, I have seen such a change, and it is for the worse. There is not much leadership being built in our workforce today. The result, in men, is when they go home, there is no leadership in their home either. Men and women are afraid to make choices or decisions at the worksite. They fear getting fired or dropped to a lower position in the company. When you do get tough with someone, while trying to teach them, their feelings sometimes get hurt and we're the one sent down the road kicking rocks, wondering what happened and thinking to ourself, *Man, back when I was learning, my boss was tough on me, he taught me my job and kept me from getting hurt and I came out all right.* Thank God he was hard on me. It built me into the leader I am today. A leader for my family. A leader for Christ in a way He would want me to lead. I lead by His example.

Proverbs 31:8-9 (NIV)
"Speak up for those who cannot speak for themselves, for the rights of all who are destitute. Speak up and judge fairly; defend the rights of the poor and needy."

When my kids were young, I had the privilege of owning my own company and having my kids work with me. I was tough on them, but I also knew when the time came to extend a kind hand. I taught my kids excellent work ethic like my dad taught me. I was able to instill into all of them about everyday life, about growing up, common sense, manners, and treating others with respect. I taught them how to stand up for those that needed it. I give my wife credit for being tough in a kind way and leading the family to God's word and His loving ways. I think some of us being tough in different situations can backfire on us easily. A story comes to mind of our kids and that there is always a right way and a wrong way to be tough. We, as parents, often find ways to always find the bad or the negative. I know because I have done this. We sometimes tend to live our dreams through our children, whether it be sports or grades that we ourselves did not excel in and in turn, we expect our kids to be the best at them. We try to make our children what we never were. After the game or event, we go over the video, telling them what or where they messed up, and how they should not have done this; or when they did not do that right. All the while, we are forgetting about extending a kind hand and just being proud and accepting who they are.

The movie 8 Seconds was based on the true story of the legendary bull rider, Lane Frost. This is a very inspiring movie with an equally sad ending that will bring a tear or two to your eyes. In the movie, Lane and his dad are watching a video of one of Lane's rides, and all he wanted from his dad was his approval and to tell him how proud he was of him. In turn, Lane's dad, also a rodeo star in his day, told Lane what he did wrong, telling him, "You're lucky the other guys rode so poorly." Now I know Lane's dad thought he was doing what he thought was right, being tough on him so he would become a better rider. All Lane wanted was approval from his dad and to hear, "Son I am proud of you, good job, I love you." I am not implying that Lane's dad was a bad father. I know he loved Lane very much and was proud of his son, I have been in the same situation with my kids as Lane's dad was. I tried to be tough and teach them to be a better person, but I was being tough the wrong way.

As parents bringing up our kids, we learn as we go. Our elders, with their wisdom, can teach us a lot about raising our children. I was always the type of dad that knew what was going on all the time. Sometimes the kids would get one by me, but my kids always knew Kim and I were there for them no matter what. They always knew they could talk to us about problems or everyday life. I remember one time; my oldest daughter Chelsea was having some issues at college and was at home on break. I made sure I was the dad that paid attention to the important things, and I knew something was going on with her. Instead of pushing and prying into her life, I gave her the space she needed till she was ready to talk, and I knew eventually she would. There was nothing the kids could not talk to Kim and myself about. They knew we were tough on right and wrong, but they also knew we had a kind hand and that we knew when to extend them.

On one of God's beautiful sunny warm afternoons, standing out in the middle of the pasture doing some work, I looked up and saw Chelsea walking toward me. She came up and gave me a hug, with tears streaming down her face, telling me about the issues in life that she was going through. I sat there just listening and being her friend and at the end, I extended my kind hand, told her it would be okay, and that mom and I loved her. I gave her some advice and prayed with her. Back then, I was not much on praying, but Chelsea told me later that this was one of her special times in life, out in that pasture, with her dad and our prayer time. Something she will cherish her whole life and me too.

As parents, we have the responsibility to raise our children as God sees fit; by His laws. There is so much we as parents can see wrong in our kids. Bad grades, talking back, not doing chores around the house, and not excelling in a particular sport to the level we would like them to. There are so many things we can find wrong, but we need to be finding all the important things our kids are doing right. We need to build them up, tell them we are proud of them every day and how much we love them and how much God loves them too. If they are messing up, remember as you're talking to them to build them up first, then at the end, very shortly, tell them where they messed up. Remember the "Cowboy way." Talk less, say more.

Back in the 5th grade, when my son Chase went out for pee wee football, I got a call from his head coach. He called because he was looking for a line coach to help. I told him, "'Well that is fine, but why are you calling me?" he said, "Because you are going to be my line coach this season," he informed me. I came back at him telling him "I don't think so buddy, I'm a wrestler, not a football player." And after an hour on the phone with him, I gave in. "Okay you win; I'll see you at practice." As I look back on my life, I can now see how God has used things, mostly the things I didn't want to do, to teach me valuable lessons and strengthening my walk with God.

Proverbs 22:6
"Train a child in the way he should go, and when he is old he will not turn from it." (NIV)

There were three dads coaching this peewee football team that year, including me. We were the Redland Chargers, and we were the youngest and smallest team in the league. I know this was God pushing me to be a coach that year, it wound up being an incredibly special time in my life, one that I will cherish in my mind and heart as long as I live. That year, as a team, we should have never won a game due to being the youngest and smallest team, but not only did we win some, we went all the way to the playoffs. Not only were we undefeated but we went to the Championship Superbowl Game! This was a David and Goliath moment when our team WON the Superbowl!

What impressed me about Jim, our head coach, was how tough he was on the boys, but he did it in such a way that he gained their trust and respect. They honestly thought they were ten feet tall and bullet proof. What Jim instilled into those young men was amazing! He always knew when to turn the toughness into a kind hand. I learned that season life lessons from the Coach and the boys. There are a reason God gives us these opportunities and what a blessing they turn out to be!

Thank God for the blessings in life and the blessings yet to come.

More Of My Story: Giving God The Reins To Your Life

JOHN 1:9

"The true light that gives light to every man was coming into the world." (NIV)

You know men, there's a time and a place in our lives when we finally start our walk with God. I tell people the worst thing you can do is shove it onto a person, because you will just push that person away from God and not to Him. Pray for that person. Plant the seed. God will take over from there. Live as God tells us to and believe me when I tell you this, that person you are praying for to come to Christ, is watching you closely. Watching how you live your life for Christ and His word. He is seeing the joy in your heart and wanting what you have. His pride and his stubbornness are getting in the way along with Satan egging him on to live for the world. One day your prayers will be answered, and that person has hit rock bottom, tired of this life, the worries, the struggles. He will look up and say, "Lord I am tired, I need you God. Please help me. I am giving you the reins to my life Lord."

This is true because I was that person, and this was my wife Kim praying for twenty-five years of our married life. Praying for me that I may come closer to the Lord. Her prayers were answered in the year 2006. Back in my younger years, I would say I was one of the biggest posers in church. I made sure that the preacher saw me so he would put that mark on the board that I was in church. But when I got out, I went back to my old ways. I do have to admit that I heard some particularly good sermons occasionally when I was paying attention.

I really was not that bad of a guy. One thing for sure, I was not living the way the Lord would want me to. My mouth was bad, I drank, and the hard-earned money I made while working was mine. Every time my wife talked about tithing, giving to God, that part I could not grasp a hold of. I figured that I made that hard-earned money on my own, every decision and venture I did was on my own. I got the things for my family they needed on my own. Who needs God? Those were my thoughts. How wrong I was! But all that time in my life, I thought I was invincible, and I did not need help from anyone, or anyone telling me what to do. Now I do not know if part of my problem was being hardheaded, and my stubbornness had anything to do with me being of Scottish blood or not. My mom was an incredibly beautiful Scottish lady, born and raised in Dundee, Scotland. My daughter Jessica reminds me a lot of my mom with her kindness and beautiful black hair. My dad was serving in the Air Force in Scotland, when he met my mom, Kathy. My brother was born in Dundee, Scotland, so there is a lot of Scottish influence in me. My parents' marriage did not last long, and we were young when they divorced.

We were taken away from our mom and lived with our dad and his new wife, which I will share more of later in the book. One night while my wife was in bed, she looked over at me and asked if I knew what my mother had told her a while back. I looked at her and said, "No telling." "Your mother told me it was easier to shoot a Scotsman than to change his mind." I kind of glared at my wife and noticed her hands under the covers, and asked her, "Honey, you don't have a pistol hidden under those covers, do you?" Smiling at me with her beautiful red hair she said, "maybe." Well without delay I had a choice to make and vowed to her, "Honey, I will do much better, I love you." It is good to have some fun and humor in your marriage. It keeps it spiced up a little. I remember back then going to Bible studies my wife would talk me into going with her. That same old feeling would creep over me, scared that they would call on me to read a verse or pray at the end of our study. I hardly ever opened my Bible, and of course, praying was out of the question. That is why I loved attending my preacher's Bible study, because Chris knew not to call on me and embarrass me. Chris knew that I wasn't quite there yet. I learned a lot from this man's teachings that I kept in the back of my mind. I respected the man for who he was. While going to these Bible studies occasionally, I entered the room and the first thing I did was scope it out to see who was there. I am Mr. Tough Guy of course, so I went in judging the men in there right away. Putting them into my category of *a bunch of wimps*.

At that time in my life, I didn't realize then that I really wasn't the tough guy I thought I was. When I was out in society or working, I didn't want anyone to know that I had gone to church, and you never heard me talk about God outside of the church that often.

John 7:13
"But no one would say anything publicly about Him for fear of the Jews." (NIV)

Everyone was talking about Jesus! But when it came time to speak up for Him in public, no one said a word. All were afraid. Fear can stifle our witness. Although many talk about Christ in church, when it comes to making a public statement about their faith, they are often embarrassed. Jesus says that He will acknowledge us before God if we acknowledge Him before others.

The verse in John really points to me and hits me hard on how I used to be. It all came down to fear. Talking about God in public, I was embarrassed. I wanted the satisfaction from the people and not God. Being around Godly people really rubbed off on me. Deep down, I wanted what they had. I just wasn't sure at that point in my life how to get it. Sometimes, Kim would sign us up as greeters, and I would also serve communion. It made me feel good inside, the little I did do for the Lord. I just didn't want to expose myself too much in the church, I was the guy that stayed to himself and remained cautious when getting involved in the activities. I respect my wife for all she has done for me and our family. She has been such a blessing and has made many sacrifices for us. I can't thank her enough. In years past, I didn't know what God had blessed me with when He gave me Kim.

Proverbs 31:12
"She brings him good, not harm, all the days of her life." (NIV)

Back then, I didn't know that Kim was bringing me good by getting me closer to the Lord any way she could. Sometimes I took it as though she was trying to harm me in a sense that she was forcing me into different things for God that I didn't really care about. As I mentioned before, Kim and I had our battles, our marriage wasn't perfect and at times, looking back now, I wouldn't have blamed my wife for leaving me. But she hung in there and kept fighting for our marriage, and for me, and my relationship with God. During our marriage, I fought a battle inside of me with my past. I will explain this later. I have realized in life that us men hate to hear the truth because it hurts. We don't want to face it. But if we do, if we listen and face the truth, no matter how bad it hurts, we will be better men. We would be the Godly men that Christ wants us to be. My mother and father-in-law had such a considerable influence on me when it came to Christ. They showed Christ's love through themselves with their caring hearts and their love. They were very understanding when I would ask questions about the Lord and share with me and took the time to explain the word to me. I always looked up to Newt and how tough he would be when needed, but how kind he could be as well. My mother-in-law, Sue was a very caring woman who had such a big heart for Christ and her family. She was the mom to me that I never had. I had a lot of incredibly special times and conversations about God with Sue. I remember a fishing trip where all of us went to Flaming Gorge in Utah, and while out on the boat, I just couldn't understand in my mind who the Holy Spirit was and how He was involved in our daily lives. So, I asked Sue. She explained to me how our lives are involved with the Holy Spirit. There were a lot of people who were extremely helpful in teaching me the word of God and Jesus, and I had a lot of questions. Before Kim and I were married, I had the privilege of having Newt baptize me at an early age in my life. It was a special time for me. Newt later told me that I was the first person he had baptized.

Mark 16:16

"Whoever believes and is baptized will be saved, but whoever does not believe will be condemned." (NIV)

Well, I figured I was starting out on the right foot by getting baptized and starting this new chapter in my life.

You look back on your life and think to yourself, *if I could go back and do it all over, would I have done things differently?* Some of us have been there and had those same thoughts. We think of the terrible things we have done and the things we are not proud of, and in our minds deep down we are thinking there is no way God will forgive us for those things. We think we are going to Hell. I have good news for you, God will forgive. Jesus died on the cross to forgive us *all* for our sins. All we must do is ask, repent, and God will forgive. On one hand, Satan is very sly at reminding us of our past, trying to get us to think how bad and useless we were. God on the other hand will forget and forgive us of our sins and never remind us of them again.

Isaiah 43:18

"Forget the former things; do not dwell on the past." (NIV)

God is a loving God. He means us no harm and wants to see us all in Heaven. I look back and see how God was really involved in my life, back in my younger days. God put the loving and Godly people in my life, especially my loving wife. I got to be honest, men, without her I wouldn't be where I am now with Christ in my life. She has been and still is such a blessing to me, and to our kids and other people who have and will come across her path. Kim is an incredibly special lady. You can feel the love of Christ in her heart. She would take the hurt of others upon herself and pray for that person, she's not afraid to show her emotions. But I could see Kim and the hurt she sometimes carries for other people. A woman who I admire very much for never giving up on me. A woman who has such a love for Christ and others. A woman I am immensely proud to call my wife, the mother to our children, my partner, my best friend, and the love of my life.

Ecclesiastes 4:12 (NIV)
"Though one may be overpowered, two can defend themselves. A cord of three strands is not quickly broken."

Kim is a very forgiving woman, and she must be to put up with me all these years of our married life. I had a very hardened heart, from my past, which I took out on my family. I am not writing this to lay blame on anyone. The biggest and hardest thing to do in life is to forgive that person or persons and the hardships they brought onto you. The only person that is not forgiving that hurt, is you. I have heard story after story of how this person cannot forgive that person that hurt him or her. Some will carry the burden of their past up to fifty years against someone who probably doesn't realize you have been holding a grudge against them, or against someone who has passed on. You know folks, Jesus died on the cross for our sins. He died for each one of us, wanting all of us to be with Him in Heaven. We all have a past. A story to tell and share, and someone to forgive that has hurt us.

Colossians 3:13

"Bear with each other and forgive whatever grievances you may have against one another. Forgive as the Lord forgave you."
(NIV)

Wisdom; the first to apologize is the bravest. The first to forgive is the strongest. And the first to forget is the happiest. Quote: Diary, Me

The Lords Way

There will come a time in every person's life when we finally give in to the Lord, some of us take longer than others. I'm one of those longer types of guys, but we will all have a choice on this earth to make the right or wrong decision. We all have a story to share, and that is especially important.

Back in December of 2005, I had surgery on my left knee. The surgery was done in Vail, Colorado, by Dr. Steadman who was known all over the country as being the best at what he does. The surgery was a success, and I didn't really realize how bad the tear was until after the surgery. I probably didn't help the injury much either by waiting so long to get it fixed.

I had to stay in the hospital overnight and the next morning, all of us were taken to the rehab room to get started on our rehab sessions so we could get the heck out of there and go home. An hour ticks by slowly as my wife and I are still sitting there waiting. I was thinking, don't forget about me guys, I need a little rehab too. A little while longer goes by, when one of the rehab personnel walks over to Kim and me and says to us, "I'm sorry, Dr. Steadman told us not to even touch you until he talks with you." This didn't sound promising to me. Another hour went by before the doctor came over. He was one of the nicest and sweetest men, and I just knew he was a Christian. We sat there together, and he told us that the injury was worse than he had thought and that no weight was to be put down on my leg for six weeks. After that, we will take another look at it and decide on therapy and go from there. I already had two other reconstructive knee surgeries in the years past and knew the down time I was going to have with this one too. I bet you're thinking to yourself, what does knee surgery have to do with this story? It has a lot to do with it. Sometimes in life, we all will endure disappointment at one time or another or several times throughout our life. We all hate disappointment, we want things to go well, and we all often have the tendency to blame God for our disappointments, making Him the object of our wrath.

Job 2:10

"He replied, "You are talking like a foolish woman. Shall we accept good from God, and not trouble?" in all this, Job did not sin in what he said." (NIV)

The book of Job is a remarkable story of a man that loved God with all his heart. A man that had it all, family, land, a beautiful house, and all kinds of livestock. Some of the things we all, or most of us anyway, dream of having for ourselves on this earth. Job was very wealthy in the money aspect. But his greatest wealth was his love for the Lord. One day, in the blink of an eye, it was all gone. Job lost his children, livestock, along with every earthly thing he had. From Job's mouth came:

Job 1:21-22

"Naked I came from my mother's womb, and naked I will depart. The LORD gave and the Lord has taken away; may the name of the Lord be praised." (NIV)

In all this, Job did not sin by charging God with the wrongdoing. Job was also hit on his health to the point that many of us could not fathom what he went through with the pain and discomfort of the sickness that was put upon him. What Job went through; I would doubt any of us will ever experience all that he endured. The book of Job is an awesome story to read and how Satan tried to turn him from God. Through his faith and love for the Lord, Satan lost the battle. This is a very evil and sinful world we live in today. A world where God gives us choices through right from wrong. These choices we are free to make but in turn what choices we make can affect us in our lives. God comes into the picture to guide us and protect us on our journey. He is checking our faith and belief in Him.

After my surgery, I thought, "Lord, I don't have time for this, I'm too busy, why me?" The Lord does not put disappointment in our lives. He is a loving God and wants us to succeed in life by following Him and loving Him with all our hearts. I feel that sickness or injuries that happen to us on this earth can be a blessing, forcing us to slow down, allowing us to get to know ourselves better and, more importantly, get to know our Heavenly Father better. You see, I was the type of guy always going a hundred miles an hour, putting God on the back burner. You get laid up, sit around the house for months, watching every movie that has come out. After a day or two of this, you start to get bored, but the last thing you want to do is pick up your Bible and read it. You know once I really started reading the Word, I loved it! It's one of the best books that you will hopefully never be finished with, a book that will get you through your struggles and disappointments. A book that teaches you how to listen to God and why you are on this earth. Next time you find yourself in disappointment, illness, surgery, or whatever it may be, use that crucial time to get to know God and yourself better.

I really think my wife was at the end of her rope and trying to get me to see God through her eyes. Kim was such a blessing to me, and I think I had about worn her completely out. What else could she do to get me closer to God? If I am being honest, I even think God was thinking, "Man, this guy is hardheaded!" Then one Sunday back in December of 2005, while at church, we were all visiting after the sermon was over, I looked at my wife across the room and thought to myself, *"Okay, zip it up and quit talking, I'm hungry!"* When unexpectedly, my brother-in-law Sean announces loud across the room, "Hey Jeff, we have this Bible study going on at breakfast every Thursday morning at some restaurant." I looked at Sean waving my arms to shut his mouth because I didn't want my wife to hear. Now, it was noisy in the room with all the conversations going on, and I don't know what you think, but it seems to me that a lady can hear five conversations going on while she is having her own conversation! I will never figure that one out… hoping she didn't hear Sean, my wife with her beautiful smile turned looking right at me and said, "That sounds fun, are you going?" All I can do is look at Sean and think," thanks *a lot, buddy, for opening your mouth.*" Later, you will see where Sean, opening his mouth and inviting me to breakfast Bible study, became a big blessing; a blessing that is going to change my life forever.

Teach Your Kids The True Word

Proverbs 22:6 (NIV)
"Train a child in the way he should go,
and when he is old he will not turn from it."

Quote – **"If we didn't teach our children to follow Christ, the world will teach them not to."**

How true this quote is, today. The world is teaching our kids to go by their rules and their principles while trying to take God out of everything, schools, government, the work force, and even out of our homes. The list goes on and on. People, we need to wake up before it is too late, our children are the future. This country was founded on Biblical beliefs, the Word of God, and we must get that back before it is too late. That starts with the future, teaching our children the true word of God.

I give credit where credit is due, and the credit goes again to my wife Kim and her mom and dad for being such great mentors with our kids on the teachings of the Lord and how to just live their lives the way God would want them to. The kids at an early age, and into young adulthood, learned the Lord's way from them. I do remember Kim and me saying their prayers at night, more my wife as she was better at it. They were not perfect, as they got older, they did things that we, as parents, didn't agree with. But let's face it, we were young once too, and did things we got into trouble for, and we had fun doing it! I think that's just part of growing into young adults. As parents, our job is to teach them right from wrong. God gave us that job to bring our children up right and more importantly, to teach them the ways of God. Kim and I have been very blessed with how our children turned out with their own walks. There were years that I had my doubts, and thought to myself," Where *did we go wrong?"* But things worked out for the good with prayer and faith. Kids watch their parents' every move, what we say, how we treat each other, and the respect we have towards others. As our children grew older, we taught them the values of life and how God created us all equal. One of my favorite quotes is, *"I am no better than that person there. I put my pants on the same way, one leg at a time, God made us all equal."*

I learned a lot of this from my dad and growing up around him. Respecting people, no matter their age, looks, or what they might have done in their past, you forgive. The one thing I really respected about my dad was his handshake, it was sincere along with his words.

While raising our children, my wife leaned more on the Bible, coming up with verses all the time on how they needed to live their lives. She did a wonderful job, and I thank her sincerely. What she instilled in our children at an early age, they carried with them in their hearts to become the men and women they are today, God's disciple's. Me on the other hand, being the man I am, I wasn't much on reading the Bible back then, but I knew right from wrong. I seemed to try and do things my way then, they were really God's way even though I wasn't quoting scriptures all the time.

We brought our children up to work hard, understand the values of life, and to respect and stand up for others when needed. My wife at times thought I was too tough on them. Mothers are like that, and you must respect them. They are like a grizzly sow; you mess with their cubs and you're going to pay. It's especially important to *show* and instruct your children. Spend quality time with them doing things and letting them do them as well. There is no greater joy than a child carrying out a project on his or her own, that you spent the time to teach them. As they're running in the house, done with their project and proudly yelling so excitedly, "Look, mom and dad, what I did!" As you smile and say, "Good job, we love you." It makes your heart feel so good. I know that God is looking upon you saying, "Good job, thank you."

Colossians 3:24 (NIV)

"Since you know that you will receive an inheritance from the Lord as a reward. It is the Lord Christ you are serving."

Proverbs 3:32 (NIV)
"For the Lord detests a perverse man but takes the upright into his confidence."

Kim and I were talking the other day on this subject. What is a Warrior? She had her version and I had mine. If you put our two versions together, it came out as a mighty man of God. I want to really emphasize Kim's version of a Warrior because she comes up with good advice being a Lady and all. Kim was talking about being a Warrior for Christ in our family, standing up for right and wrong, giving your word and standing by it, putting God first in all things, honesty and showing Gods love to brothers and sisters. Today's world is getting worse and worse with all the technology out there, computers, cell phones, video games, and a lot more I haven't mentioned. Don't get me wrong, technology is good, but it is how we use it in today's world.

This life is full of battles. Threats to our faith are always present and as Christians, our fight is against the powers of this world that call us away from God. The good news is that we have every weapon we need at our disposal." When we put on the Armor of God's Word remember that Jesus goes with us, we can face down every enemy and rest assured that we will come out victorious." Written by Jada Pryor

2 Samuel 10:12 (NIV)
"Be strong and let us fight bravely for our people and the cities of our God. The Lord will do what is good in His sight."

Compared to when I was a kid, it has gotten bad in the world today. The end of time is close. To be honest, I would hate to be raising kids today. But while I am still on this earth, I am going to be a Warrior for God sharing our family values with our grown kids and grandchildren. I compare our children with a young horse. Bringing up a young colt and teaching him respect for the reins has a lot to do with how we raise our children. First, when a young horse comes of age, we must start working with them. Now, if we left that young colt out to pasture until he was a lot older and grown into a mature horse, he is going to develop some rude habits. Habits that are going to be tough to break. So, at an early age, we start teaching and doing preparation work on them so he will remember what he has learned when he becomes older. Before breaking a young colt, you must build trust, then confidence, and be stern in a way that they must respect you but also feel the love in you for them. You must keep teaching and loving this horse while he is coming up in maturity. If you don't, he will go back to his rude habits and then you will have your hands full getting him back the right way. I was talking to Kim, and she mentioned to me that now days, all our kids must do is hit three buttons on their cell phones or computers and boom, a porn site comes up. Our kids also play so many video games and some of those games have so much killing in them and these kids are getting a thrill out of that. This, in turn, will start to develop a dark side in them. I really don't think they meant for all the bad to develop when the first computer was made. This is an evil world we live in and in my opinion, Satan saw an open door with the technology and walked right into people's minds, bringing filth and corruption into our society.

"We should never let corruption, which is a scheme from Satan cause us to lose focus from Christ. We are not to let it cause us to make excuses. Even though corruption is all around us, Let's walk by the spirit and continue to grow in Christ."
Information from echurchgiving.com

"The world's corruption is a result of its defiance."
Warren Wierbe

Isaiah 1:4 (NIV)

‘Ah, sinful nation, a people loaded with guilt, a brood of evil-doers, children given to corruption! They have forsaken the LORD; they have spurned the Holy one of Israel and turned their backs on him.”

The world today is telling our kids don't worry, we forgive you, that's the way you were born, all they are doing is giving them a one – way ticket to Hell. It really hurts my heart, on the corruption in our school system. Today, being a teacher is tough, these kids know they can get away with murder and the teachers can't do anything about it. And of course, we blame the kids. It is not the kid's fault, it is the parent's fault, they are not raising them according to God's law. Sometimes, I think it should be the parents on trial, not the kids, we might have a change in attitude from the parents then. There are so many single moms out there, trying to raise their kids the right way and holding down a job. I might get a lot of criticism saying this being the Christian I am today, but we have a lot of dead-beat dads out there that really don't care about their kids. Men, you might be separated or divorced or having a child out of wedlock but be men and stand up for what is right for your family. You have a responsibility for yourself, your kids, and for God. God gives you something so precious and you don't take it upon yourselves to love and cherish and to teach that child the ways of the Lord. As parents, we have a huge responsibility with our children. Teaching them right from wrong. Teaching them respect, responsibility, and the way of life according to God's law. Back when Kim and I started having children, (it was a shock to my married life, my wife wasn't just mine anymore, I had to share her with my kids). My father-in-law told me, "The honeymoon is over once the kids show up." The first child is a big shock to your life, but it is also such a blessing from God. Who can say there is not a God when you see a baby born? It is one of God's biggest miracles in my opinion. When we started having more children and our family grew, I made a deal with Kim, I wanted her to be a stay-at-home mom and raise our kids, and that I would do whatever it took to make that happen. I am not in any way trying to tell moms to stay home or putting you down if you don't stay home to raise your kids. In today's world, both parents usually must work to make ends meet. Back then, Kim and I were blessed to be able to let her stay home. I was working a lot of overtime, eighty to ninety hours a week, but we always had food on the table, a roof over our heads, and clothes on our backs. Who could ask for anything more? God poured the blessings in, and I did without on material things to make sure that my family was taken care of. A lot of people, when I tell them this don't believe me, but Kim and I had such a tight budget that if we were lucky, we might be able to afford to take our kids out to breakfast after church or to dinner once a month on the budget we lived on. We had precious time at home around the dinner table being a family. Even today, all our meals are still served at home, spending quality time together. Restaurants don't always offer that personal atmosphere. It blows my mind that any day of the week, you can drive by any restaurant downtown and see how packed they are. I think to myself, *doesn't anyone cook and eat at home anymore?* When we go to the restaurant, which is not often, it is such a treat for us. It gives my wife a break and sometimes we might throw a movie into our date night. We are so close to our kids, not just mom and dad to them but we have become their friends. We are someone they trust to share their concerns and trials with. Someone who will always tell them, 'We love you.' Someone who taught them the Good Word, and someone who, if it ever came to it, would lay their life down for them.

Ephesians 4:29 (ESV)

"Let no corrupting talk come out of your mouths, but only such as is good for building up, as fits the occasion, that it may give grace to those who hear."

One of my favorite Christian Comedians is Ken Davis. When I watched one of his first comedy acts on video, I was laughing so hard it brought tears to my eyes. What amazed me about this man is his story coming up as a child to a young man and later in his life. He becomes one of God's disciples. He shares his story and does it in a way that is funny, but the truth and his main point (especially to kids) is that God made you who you are for a reason. He made you special, formed you in your mother's womb, with plans for a great future for you. Ken talks about his life coming up in High School and never having a date with a girl his whole high school career. Ken had a disease that affected him being able to hold his hands straight and grabbing something. He tells the story of going out for football one year and during drills at practice, he kept trying to catch the football and he never could do it due to his disease. There was one time, the coach kept watching him miss catching the ball and walked up to him and said, "Go hit the showers, you'll never amount to anything." What a blow Ken took hearing those words from the coach. That would hurt any kid being told something like that. But Ken didn't let that stop him and his love for the Lord, Ken is a motivational speaker today. Like he says, "God made you special for a reason."

Proverbs 31:26 (ESV)
"She opens her mouth with wisdom, and the teaching of kindness is on her tongue."

Parents, teachers, coaches, and other superior positions, that as grown-ups, we partake in, in society today, are especially important. What comes from our tongue can be very devastating to a child or a young adult. Now I am not saying don't make your children mind, but you can do it in a way that still gains their respect. We have all been there and have said words that we regret, wishing we could take them back. We put wounds on our children that take a long time to heal just because we spoke before we thought. The tongue is an immensely powerful tool, how we use it can either bring someone up or cause irreparable damage. It is especially important that we tame our tongues before we speak.

I know I have written a lot about teaching our children the true word, but this is especially important and a crucial part of this book. Our kids are the future and without them being taught wisdom, right from wrong, and God's Word there will be no future. So just bear with me, what I am writing comes from experience. Watching how the world is changing so fast scares me. We all know that God is in control, and we must work hard getting Him back into this country. I don't mean that God is not here, God has always been here. It's just that we have gotten to the point where we have quit inviting Him where He is needed. Years ago, I was speaking at one of our W.A.H.M. breakfast meetings, and the subject I was speaking about was our children. When I finished, several men came up to me, shook my hand, and thanked me for sharing. They let me know it opened their hearts up and how they now had a different outlook on their own kids. I looked straight up and said, "Thank you Lord. The glory goes to you." While I was talking to the brother's I told them that it is so easy as parents to put our kids down and sometimes we don't even know we are doing it. We can easily find so many things wrong with them, where we need to look at the positive more than the negative. All these things can relate to even being an employer with employees, too.

You can put a kid down so hard by telling them what they haven't done right or what they have done wrong. We, as parents, must teach these things, but it is how we speak to them that can have damaging effects. When a child is put down so hard, it's afterwards that the child or young adult will feel worthless; that they are not good enough in this life to carry out anything. As they grow older with these feelings of self-doubt, they may turn to drugs and gangs. They may or think about committing suicide. They may go to some other environment where they feel they are wanted and not put down all the time. All these usually end in disaster. We always ask ourselves, where did I go wrong?

Numbers 6:24-26 (NIV)
"The LORD bless you and keep you; The LORD make His face shine upon you and be gracious to you; The LORD turn His face toward you and give you peace."

I want to share a story about my youngest daughter, Jessy, that I hope explains what I am talking about. Years ago, my daughter was going to college and after about a year, her grades weren't up to par. I think she was enjoying college life in a separate way than what she should have been doing. My wife, mad and upset about the situation, told me to deal with her. So, I called Jessy and told her, let's meet for lunch, I need to talk to you. I know Jessy well enough, and she knew what I was going to talk to her about. I bet she had a stomachache driving down to meet me because when us dads get involved, we are serious. I have to say, that was one of the best lunches I have had with my daughter. So, when I got home, Kim wanted to know every detail. It's funny how women are like this. Us men would be like, "How was your lunch?" "Oh good." And that's all that would have been said and we would have gone on with our day. But our wives, you better plan to talk about it for at least an hour. So, Kim wanted to know what we talked about. I told her for the whole lunch hour I talked to Jessy about how proud we both were of her and the accomplishments in life she had made. We were proud of how far she had come in her faith and love for God. While I paid the ticket and we were walking out the door, I looked at Jessy and said, "Honey, your mom and I really care about you and love you dearly, but your homework isn't all that good, let's see what you can do about that." She smiled and said, "Thank you, dad, I love you both." Like the old Cowboy saying goes, 'Talk less, say more.' Now I could have gone to that lunch with her and for that whole hour chewed on her butt on the negative things in her life. She would have left their feeling like a piece of horse crap that somebody stomped flat and that she was worthless. Instead, I built her up and gave her confidence and pride in herself and she knew she was loved unconditionally and that someone cared.

John 13:34-35 (NIV)
"A new command I give you: Love one another. As I have loved you, so you must love one another."

The Start Of A New Life

2 CORINTHIANS 5:17 (NIV)

"Therefore, if anyone is in Christ, he is a new creation; the old has gone, the new has come!"

Finding my Identity
Our Identity Should be based on how God sees us.

Christians are brand-new people on the inside, The Holy Spirit gives them new life, and they are not the same anymore. We are not reformed, rehabilitated, or reeducated – we are recreated (new creations) living in a vital union with Christ.

Colossians 2:6-7 (NIV)
"So then, just as you received Christ Jesus as Lord, continue to live in Him, rooted and built up in Him, strengthened in the faith as you were taught, and overflowing with thankfulness."

Continuing my story: When Kim and I left the church, all she could talk about was the breakfast Bible study that Sean mentioned, or should I say opened his big mouth about. Kim thought that it sounded so awesome and kept asking me if I was going to go. I kept telling her, "No, I am not going, so be quiet about it." Those of you who know my wife once she gets something in that head of hers, she will keep nagging at you like an old mean bull chasing you around the corral until you finally give in. I look back on this now and I figured, this was Kim's last hope of getting me close to the Lord. Sunday night, Monday night, Tuesday night, and Wednesday night, Kim would not leave me alone or shut up about this Bible breakfast study. These breakfasts were every Thursday morning starting at 6AM. I thought to myself, who in their ever-loving mind would get up at 5AM, get ready, and be there by 6 just to hear a bunch of Bible thumpers? It just didn't make sense to me. Come Wednesday night, Kim asked me one more time if I was going to go. I told her I would, just to get her to shut up about it, all the while thinking to myself, I'll just go this one time to make Kim happy and then she'll drop it. I had forgotten how persistent my wife was though. I was in for a shocking surprise that I didn't see coming.

Thursday morning came around, I wish I could say bright and early, but I am going to say dark and early. I got dressed without saying a word to Kim, walking out the door, she said with that big, beautiful smile, "I love you." I grumbled back, "I love you too." Believe me, I was not a happy camper. I go to this restaurant called Good Pastures (any ole cowboy would like that name; makes you feel right at home on the range). I walked into one of the conference rooms where they were holding this event and glancing around the room, I noticed there were around fifteen men. I was uncomfortable walking into that room with everybody staring at me. I felt like a sheep coming to the wolves' den for the kill. I made it through the breakfast Bible study but couldn't make it out of there fast enough. Not even giving my brother-in-law the time of day because I was still mad at him for opening his mouth.

Proverbs 3:5-6 (NIV)

"Trust the Lord with all your heart and lean not on your own understanding; In all your ways acknowledge Him, and He will make your paths straight."

Driving back home, I was glad that it was over and figured I did my good deed for my wife by going. When I walked into the house, Kim wanted to know everything, who was there, what did they talked about, and the big question, was I going again? First, I told her I only knew one guy besides my brother-in-law Sean. I had no idea what they were talking about, and I was not going again. Remember me telling you how persistent my wife was. Well, she wouldn't leave me alone about going to another one. I was hoping some job would come up out of town so she would leave me alone about it. Then the Thursday after that rolled around and I'm dragging my butt out of bed, again, to go. My wife was obsessed with these breakfast Bible studies. She started to sound like a broken record player, over and over, "Are you going again?" After about my fifth breakfast, there were more men coming to this event. This Bible study was started by several men, but the main man, Randy VanConett had the vision after attending a Christian Camp over by Denver, Colorado, and Randy is the founder of the ministry that is called Warrior at Heart Ministry in Grand Junction, Colorado. What I didn't know was they had already put on several camps up in God's beautiful wilderness, holding them at resort lodges. The breakfast they held every Thursday morning was the icing on the cake.

When I started seeing more men coming to these breakfasts, I noticed they were tough looking dudes. These were men I wouldn't want to mess with, they were my kind of men, Warriors. Someone I figured I would trust watching my back in battle while I was watching theirs. I started thinking about this, "Why were these tough looking men here?" I thought this Christianity thing was for wimps. How wrong I was, *again.* I was beginning to get excited about breakfast and seeing the "brothers." Unbelievably, after a while, I started reminding my wife about them and to make sure the coffee pot was set Thursday morning at 5AM. I know Kim was excited that I was enjoying Bible study and probably praying that I would stick with it, hoping and praying that my heart would get softened and closer to God.

John 8:12 (NIV)

When Jesus spoke again to the people, He said, "I am the light of the world. Whoever follows Me will never walk in darkness, but will have the light of life."

"When we walk with the Lord, we draw closer to Him with all our heart. He becomes our focus. Our hearts long for Him and seek His presence. Our desire to have fellowship with Christ and to be like Him will grow while our worldly desires decrease."
Biblereasons.com

As time went on, I asked my youngest son Chase if he wanted to come with me one week to the Warrior breakfast and he said, "Sure, why not Dad." We both had a wonderful time, and he would go with me whenever he could. There was something about W.A.H.M. that really touched my heart. It was different than any other religious activity that I had ever been involved in. This was a ministry for us men to get together in prayer, share out story, and build us into leaders God intended us to be for our family and church and to go out and spread the good word. We all had our own churches we went to on Sundays to hear the teachings from the preacher, which we needed as well. W.A.H.M. taught us to become better men, Warriors for Christ, and the loving husbands and fathers we were intended to be. Going to the breakfasts is where I met my good friend, Craig Bowen. I remember the first time he walked through the door. He was younger than me and someone you wouldn't want to be on his bad side. This man was all Warrior, but it didn't bother me. I sized him up and really thought to myself, *I wonder how tough this guy really is? I bet I could whip him.* I was a tough guy in my day, but I made the right choice by becoming a close friend to Craig. I told the brothers later that Craig was lucky I decided to be his friend, so he didn't have to see how tough I really was. With the brothers laughing and saying, "We would like to see that Rippy, but our bets are on Craig." I thought to myself, man, no faith in this old man here. It would have been like the David and Goliath story. Through the years, Craig and I went to a lot of Warrior camps together, cattle drives, and times we just sat together visiting and praying for each other and our families and friends. I know Craig would take a bullet for me, no questions asked, as I would do the same for him. It was God's hand meeting Craig and becoming close friends.

Colossians 3:12-14 (NIV)
"Therefore, as God's chosen people, holy and dearly loved, clothe yourselves with compassion, kindness, humility, gentleness and patience. Bear with each other and forgive whatever grievances you may have against one another. Forgive as the Lord forgave you. And over all these virtues put on love, which binds them all together in perfect unity."

Early in my life, I had friends, but getting into the ministry, I realized what faithful friends were. They were friends you trusted with your life, friends you could tell the details of your life, your issues, your wounds, who would listen and care, without judging you on where you messed up in life and would love you for who you are. They were God's disciples, God's warriors. Brothers that had a heart for God. Brothers that would walk the walk all the way with you.

Always Finish What You Start, Remember, A Handshake And A Man's Word Is As Good As A Written Contract

Genesis 47:28-31 (NIV)

"Jacob lived in Egypt seventeen years, and the years of his life were a hundred and forty-seven. When the time drew near for Israel to die, he called for his son Joseph and said to him, If I have found favor in your eyes, put your hand under my thigh and promise that you will show me kindness and faithfulness. Do not bury me in Egypt, but when I rest with my fathers, carry me out of Egypt and bury me where they are buried. I will do as you say, he said. Swear to me, he said. Then Joseph swore to him, and Israel worshiped as he leaned on top of his staff."

Putting a hand under the thigh was a sign of making a promise, much like shaking hands today. Jacob had Joseph promise to bury him in his homeland. Few things are written in this culture, so a person's word then carried as much force as a written contract today. People today seem to find it easy to say, "I didn't mean that." God's people, however, are to speak the truth and live the truth. Let your words be as binding as a written contract. Back in the old west days, there wasn't much of a written contract. The cowboy lived the "Code of the West" and that was when you didn't back out of a deal, or you ended up paying the consequences and that was something no cowboy ever wanted to face. When a cowboy signed on with an outfit, driving cattle across the country to market, he always finished what he started. Sealed the deal with his word and a handshake, given to the trail boss. Quitting along the way, leaving the outfit shorthanded, was considered cowardliness and a cowboy no one would ever trust. I guess I would call that cowboy black balled as word would get around to other outfits not to hire him because of his deed. In the movie Lonesome Dove, that I mentioned earlier, Gus was on his death bed looking at Call and asking him to bury him back in Texas under the tree next to the little creek where he and Clare spent special time together. Call, looking back at Gus said, "Are you crazy? That's a thousand miles back there.

We just got to Montana, and you want me to take you back there to Texas." Gus barely able to speak said "Yes, give me your word that you'll do it." Call stood there for a minute thinking to himself, not wanting to but caring too much for Gus. "You have my word. I'll take you back to Texas and bury you." Gus didn't have a second thought that Call wouldn't follow through, he knew his word was as good as gold. Gus passed away, and winter set in, so they put Gus into a safe place to wait till spring to start the journey. One of the ole cowboys told Call, "Don't worry if you don't make it back, we'll give him a proper burial." Call looking at the ole Cowboy, dead in the eye said, "Why would I do that, I gave him my word." "Lots of people give their word and don't follow through." The old cowboy came back to Call. As Call mounted his horse, he looked at the old timer and said, "I'll be back in the spring." And rode off to Montana. Call came back in the spring and hauled Gus back to Texas, buried him where he asked, Call kept his word. He finished what he started on the long tough journey by giving his word.

Times have changed dramatically since I was young and growing up. I remember back then, always watching my dad shaking hands as his word to other men, telling them he would do a job, giving his word and getting it done with nothing wrote on a single piece of paper. I'm not saying all deals went a hundred percent good. I've seen my dad get shafted, but in his conscience, he went through with his word and could live with that. I was brought up this way and to this day, I still go by my word and handshake. Kim and I have raised our family the same way, the way the Lord would want us to be.

Psalm 119:11 (NIV)
"I have hidden your word in my heart that I might not sin against you."

Hiding (keeping) God's word in our hearts is a deterrent to sin. This alone should inspire us to memorize scripture. But memorizing alone will not keep us from sin; we must also put God's word in our lives, making it a vital guide for everything we do. Raising our own children through their school years, we taught them and were extremely strict about when you start something, you finish it no matter how tough it gets. It builds integrity. Now, there were times they wanted to quit and take the uncomplicated way out. We would in a loving way build them up to give them the confidence they needed to keep going and in the end with a smile, they would say, "I did it!" I had many men tell me that they really respected my sons over their handshake. Nowadays, you don't see youngsters shaking hands, they are not brought up that way anymore. Today's younger generation do chest bumps instead of handshakes. I always say, you can tell a man's integrity based on his firm handshake and look you straight in the eye as to whether you could trust him or not.

During my wrestling career in High School, I wrestled varsity all four years. I loved wrestling and would not trade my High School days for anything. Wrestling is a tough sport. It is an individual sport, with no help from teammates. What you put into it is what you get out of it. You're on your own when you're out there on the mat and if you get into trouble, on your back getting pinned, you don't have much time to mess around. Now you can take the effortless way out and let the Ref slap the mat and be pinned. Or you can finish what you started in the beginning of the match when you shake hands and the whistle blows, finish what you start, the grueling six minutes giving it a hundred and ten percent, knowing you gave it your all no matter what the outcome, so when you walk off the mat, you can hold your head high, win or lose. Shaking the other wrestler's hand, looking him in the eye, now that builds integrity.

Proverbs 11:3
"The integrity of the upright guides them, but the unfaithful are destroyed by their duplicity." (NIV)

The picture above is a special, spiritual, and close friend of mine. Pat Ralston, who is a fine example of a Warrior, a leader, and a man of integrity. A man who always finishes what he starts and goes by his word and his handshake. Pat and his wife Chrisy have been great mentors to both Kim and me. A man I look up to and would risk my life for. This picture is of a ride we started in September of 2015, 'The Ride for the Lord.' Pat was the first one to go with me on this cross-country ride. He also helped me set it up. What impressed me about this man was he gave me his word to go and had not been on a horse for twenty years. We rode over grueling mountain tops 12,000' feet high, riding for four straight days and he never complained once. Pat finished what he started to the end.

Numbers 30:2 (NIV)
"When a man makes a vow to the LORD or takes an oath to obligate himself by a pledge, he must not break his word but must do everything he said."

1 John 2:5 (NIV)
"But if anyone obeys his word, God's love is truly made complete in Him. This is how we know we are in Him."

I have been in business most of my life and started up a Hydro-Ex company with these Super Sucker Trucks back in the year 2000. I remember one time going out and looking at a job jetting an irrigation line for a private individual. After figuring what the job would take to do, I gave my price to this man to do it. We agreed, and the next day, the crew and I went out and did the job. Well, it took longer than I thought, and after we got done, the gentleman was nervous about the final cost. He looked at me with concern in his eyes and said, "What do I owe you? It took longer than we thought, not being able to see the unknown." I looked back at him and said, "Whatever we agreed on yesterday when I looked at the job. It's whatever I told you, I go by my word." That man was so excited and shook my hand and told me, "Thank you, not many people go by their word anymore, you're one of the few that do." When you treat others with respect, finish what you start, and go by your word, you can feel good about yourself. When you put your head down on that pillow at night having a clear conscience, knowing in your mind you did right and, more importantly, you did right in God's eyes. Every day in our lives, we face so many obstacles with family, work, friends, strangers, church, and so on. So many people today seem to find it so easy to say, "I'll do that, you have my word." And they never follow through. Jesus gave every one of us His word, dying on the cross and forgiving us of our sins. The promise of an eternity in Paradise if we just believe in Him and accept Him as our Savior. Life on earth is tough, especially being Christian. We must stand up for each other. When the time comes one day and you start your walk with God, always remember to "Finish what you start." Don't quit halfway on God and don't quit on yourself. When you give God your word, stick with it. God will never give up on us. He gave us his word and will finish what he started.

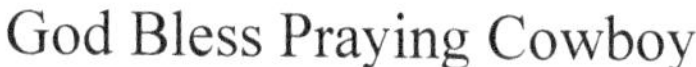

God Bless Praying Cowboy

When I tell you about my past, it is not so you feel sorry for me. I tell you because I want you to know what Jesus delivered me from. God uses all our broken pieces to make somcthing beautiful. God is making something beautiful out of you.

My First Warrior Camp

Warrior at Heart Ministry

"Battling to heal and free men's hearts by inspiring and developing men to become the leaders and stewards God intended us to be, through the power of Christ's love."

Exodus 15:3 (NIV)
"The LORD is a Warrior; the LORD is His Name."

Later in the year of 2006, going to most of the Warrior Breakfasts, my brother-in-law Sean came up to me and said, "Hey, Jeff, we have this Warrior Camp thing coming up in August if you want to go." With a stern look I said, "Sean, what more do you and my wife want from me? I am going to the Warrior breakfast, aren't you happy?" Sean commented, "Well, Jeff, you don't have to go." Being curious I asked "Sean, where is this camp and what's it about?" "It's at Camp Red Cloud in Lake City, Colorado, and to be honest, Jeff, it's hard to explain about the camp, but you need to go to and find out for yourself, if you want to. But I guarantee it will change your life."

Psalm 16:11 (NIV)

"You have made known to me the path of life; you will fill me with joy in your presence, with eternal pleasures at your right hand."

Well, I thought about it awhile and told Sean, "Okay, I'll go. Under one condition." "What's that?" Sean asked. "I'll go if I can bring my own horses, I am not going to ride some dude horse at camp, so that's the deal. If you and my wife want me to go so bad, make it happen." I didn't find out till several years later that the Camp Red Cloud leaders took two weeks to decide if they wanted my horses up there, because they didn't know me or my horses. It was a big liability, and getting sued came to their minds, but that never crossed mine. Hey, if you fall off your horse, which a cowboy will never admit to unless he's been hitting the flask too much, you'll never do that again. If you get thrown or bucked off that horse, what do you do? It's simple, you get right back on, you don't let him beat you. Kind of like life, we get thrown down, beat up, tossed around, some will quit when it gets tough, others get right back up. That's the time in our lives we must "Cowboy up" and go for it.

Psalm 13:5-6 (NIV)

"But I trust in your unfailing love; my heart rejoices in your salvation. I will sing to the LORD, for He has been good to me."

I really know it was God putting into Camp Red Cloud staff's minds to let me bring my horses to camp. God really wanted me up there. When Sean called me and said, "Camp Red Cloud decided you could bring your horses if you get a Vet-Check." I was thinking to myself, *Dang it, now I must go.* When the day came to leave for camp, we got packed up, and Chase (my son) and I headed out. While driving to camp, Chase and I got to talk about what we got ourselves into. I didn't like being around folks or the conversation too much. We were told this camp was awesome and would change our lives. I told Chase that at least we had the horses, and we could saddle up and ride all day, getting away from everyone. But like I said before, God had other plans and they weren't like my plans.

1 Corinthians 2:9-10 (NIV)
"However, as it is written: No eye has seen, no ear has heard, no mind has conceived what God has prepared for those who love him, but God has revealed it to us by His spirit."

So, we get to camp, walk in, get checked in and find a bed. After getting organized, we went to check things out. Number one – this was a beautiful lodge and everyone was nice, and they were bending over backwards to help in any way they could. You really felt at home up there and it felt good. We ran into one of the camp's directors, Kade. A genuinely nice man, originally from Texas. I didn't hold that against him being a Texan and all. (LOL) While we were talking to Kade, he said that they had been praying for some-one's nephew Jarrod, who had been kicked in the chest by a young horse and it was a severe, serious accident. In that accident, the horse wasn't intentionally trying to kick Jarrod, he just happened to be in the wrong place. Had he been anywhere else, it would have missed him, but God has other plans for this young man. Kade didn't know that Jarrod was my nephew. That's when it hit me, the power of prayer and caring, when Kade said they had been praying every day for this young man, who I loved. When I told him that Jarrod was my nephew and Chase's cousin, he was shocked. I really wasn't the praying type of guy, but that really touched my heart, knowing that all the Camp Red Cloud staff had been praying for Jarrod. I was thinking to myself, man, they don't even know Jarrod, yet they cared enough for him to take their time to pray for him, that blew my mind! I had never been around brothers that cared for me and others so much, it felt good.

Psalm 4:3 (NIV)

"Know that the LORD has set apart the Godly for Himself; the Lord will hear when I call to Him."

As the camp got going, Thursday after dinner, we all met in the main room and started with what we all had come for, to make better men of us. I was shocked when we started the session, it was not what I expected. The whole weekend we would be going through and watching videos of Wild at Heart, by John Eldredge.

Psalm 34:8 (NIV)

"Taste and see that the Lord is good; blessed is the man who takes refuge in Him."

Lean On Your Band Of Brothers As The Disciples Leaned On Jesus

Acts 1:14 (NIV)

"They all joined together constantly in prayer, along with the women and Mary the mother of Jesus, and with His brothers."

This is an important subject about leaning on your brothers when you start your walk with God and your journey through this life. You cannot do it by yourself, you will fail. You must have loving, caring, warrior brothers to get you through your walk with God. Our walk with God will last a lifetime. Being in Warriors, and the years I have been involved, I realized a person cannot and will not do it on their own. We must have brothers to help us and to help them in return. I really feel hurt in my heart for brothers that don't have anyone to lean on, to share their problems with someone to sit and listen to and pray with them. A brother that will watch your back in battle and take a bullet if it came down to it.

Ecclesiastes 4:9-10 (NIV)

"Two are better than one, because they have a good return for their work: If one falls down, his friend can help him up. But pity the man who falls and has no one to help him up!"

This verse is so true. In my own life, I have fallen so hard, and no one was there to pick me up, no one to talk to, share my wounds with, to love me and care for me, until the blessed day I met the love of my life, Kim.

There are so many bands of brother groups that watch out for each other and care for one another. I am friends with several Policemen and just being around them and listening to them, they have an extraordinarily strong brotherhood with each other, as with our Servicemen, Firefighters, and those in the workforce, this list can go on and on of brotherhoods. I can't forget about the women, the sisterhood they share with each other is powerful. I think women lean on each other more than us men do. Sometimes us men can be to macho and don't want to show weakness. My wife Kim has close friends along with her family that she will lean on and share her issues with, in return, she is there for them to lean on her. I have also leaned on Kim a lot going through trials, as she has with me. Until I got into the Warrior at Heart Ministry, I really didn't know what it meant to lean on a band of brothers. I had friends of course, but when I had problems in my life, I took care of them on my own. That's how I was brought up. I guess I didn't know any better, or I didn't know what to do.

Proverbs 17:17 (NIV)
"A friend loves at all times, and a brother is born for adversity."

I have had several brothers that were walking with God and decided that life was more fun going the other way. They were headed for destruction, but deep down they knew they were doing wrong. Occasionally, they would head back in the right direction, to God. I had a conversation with some of these men, and they would tell me maybe they should go back to church and their walk with God. I would tell them, "Buddy, that's your choice and only yours. If you decide to go back on your walk, promise me one thing, that you will use a brother to walk with you or you won't make it." You cannot do it by yourself, you need a brother or brotherhood to help each other. Jesus had his disciples and each one of them leaned on each other to get them through the good and tough times in life, but most importantly, the disciples leaned on Jesus.

1 John 3:16 (NIV)
"This is how we know what love is: Jesus Christ laid down His life for us. And we ought to lay down our lives for our brothers."

One reason for drafting this book is I see a lot of men hurting out there and nowhere to turn, nowhere to go, no one cares as to what that person is going through. It seems we're too busy to get ourselves involved in someone else's issues. If Jesus was that way, we would all really be in trouble.

In my first twenty years growing up, I never really had a person come up to me and share with me about God or invite me to church. Maybe they feared me or didn't really have time to reach out. We believers are in our comfort zone. We think, so and so will do the work. We go to church, do our charitable deeds, and go to breakfast or lunch afterwards. We then head home to relax and get ready for the work week. Have you ever thought while at breakfast or lunch, your waiter or server is hurting inside and doesn't know God or where to turn to. Thinking to themselves, "Man, I wish someone would invite me to church, they look so happy." We are too busy to pay attention or even care, or perhaps, we're scared of what they may say. What's the worst that can happen? They tell you, "No." I know all this because I was that person. Go to church, leave, and never talk about God all week until the next Sunday. I also figured back then that there were enough God-fearing people to do the Lord's work, and I didn't really have the time. But today in my walk, and with my brothers to lean on, life is now different. There is hardly a day that goes by that something isn't mentioned about God and His word. The doors open now for me, with non-believers and I am given the opportunity to share and plant the seed, then I let God take over. Today's statistics say that of all the people that attend church every week that only 5% of those believers will ever reach out to a non-believer after walking out their church doors. And of all those believers only 15% of them will ever do Gods work out outside the church doors in His wilderness. Pretty low statistics for the One that created us on this earth.

John 13:34-35 (NIV)

"A new command I give you: Love one another. As I have loved you, so you must love one another. By this all men will know that you are my disciples, if you love one another."

I love watching cowboy movies, but the sad thing is the making of cowboy movies are going down in the polls. Our younger generations like to watch these far-fetched movies that in my opinion, don't really make sense. How the West was won back then, is our heritage, our brotherhood, and God was extraordinarily strong back then. Cowboys of the olden days and cowboys of today have a strong brotherhood with each other, usually with the Lord guiding each one of them. Still, one of my favorites Is the movie, Lonesome Dove. Yes, I know it is just a movie, but if you really pay attention to the parts in it, you see strong brotherhood throughout the whole movie with a lot of good points and wisdom. The movie Comanche Moon, prelude to Lonesome Dove, shows Gus and Call starting out as Texas Rangers with their brothers riding alongside them. The movie shows, throughout their lives, how each of them grew older and developed such a strong bond for each other. Each is willing to take that bullet from bandits or an arrow from the Comanche to protect their brother. Cowboys then had a lot of hardships, a brother getting killed, doing his job, would be carried with them throughout their life. They carried the brotherhood within them. Today, I feel that the brotherhood is not as strong as it was then. This is something that needs to be put back into our lives today. If we build that strong brotherhood with each other the way it used to be, along with God, it would be tough to be taken down.

Romans 12:10 (NIV)
"Be devoted to one another in brotherly love. Honor one another above yourselves."

The Wound

Isaiah 53:5 (NIV)

"But He was pierced for our transgressions, He was crushed for our iniquities; the punishment that brought us peace was upon Him, and by His wounds we are healed."

This will be the toughest part of the writing of this book, but I feel in my heart, it is the most important and influential part. Every man, whether they know it or not, carries a wound of their past, in their heart. Some men will tell you they don't have a wound, but, they have not searched their heart or soul deep enough. Most wounds men carry can be of their childhood, their upbringing, over a friend, family member, school, sports or work. There are so many things, as a man, that we carry as a wound. We don't realize how that wound affects us, our family, and the ones we love. God is there to take that wound and heal us if we would just give it to Him. Us men, are tough, we tell ourselves that we are good, we don't have wounds, and everything is perfect. Down deep inside, we are hurting in our hearts. Our pride gets in the way, and we tell ourselves, *who am I going to share my wound with that will listen and care? No one.* So, we keep thinking *I'm fine,* but we are not.

2 Chronicles 26:16 (NIV)
"But after Uzziah became powerful, his pride led to his downfall. He was unfaithful to the Lord his God and entered the temple of the Lord to burn incense on the altar of incense."

What I tell you is a fact because that was me. Carrying a tough wound for the first twenty-five years of my married life, hurting my family and friends of whom I dearly loved. My wife would try to talk to me about my childhood, but I wouldn't have anything to do with it, especially telling a woman about my past as a child. Once again, my pride got in the way. Brothers, you know us men hate to hear the truth about our wounds, about the past, because deep down, it hurts. But if we listen, and hear the truth, and share that wound, it makes us better men. Men, to do God's work for His Kingdom, we must have a clear mind, we need to have forgiveness for those that have hurt us, and most of all, we need to have God deep in our hearts. Love Him and get to know Him better. To all the men out there that are hurting down deep with a wound, find a brother or Ministry group to share your wound with and the forgiveness that needs to be done.

"Don't allow your wounds to turn you into a
person that you are not."
Paulo Coelho

Philippians 4:8 (NIV)
"Finally, brothers, whatever is true, whatever is noble, whatever is right, whatever is pure, whatever is lovely, whatever is admirable-if anything is excellent or praiseworthy-think about such things."

Without God, Warrior at Heart Ministry, and the John Eldredge camps, none of this would have been in the making of this book and what I am about to share with you all. At these camps, we go through the John Eldredge videos and the Wild at Heart book, written by John Eldredge. I need to tell you all if it wouldn't have been for God and Warrior Heart Ministry, I don't know where I would be today. What I do know is that it wouldn't have been good, and I thank God along with my close friend Randy VanConett, who had the vision and dream to get the ministry going. Randy, as I mentioned, is the founder of Warrior at Heart Ministry. Thousands of lives have been changed and saved through the Wounded Heart. Leadership has been developed in so many men, in so many ways.

What I love about this ministry is that we are not a church, of course we share the Word of God, which is number one in Warriors, but the main goal is rescuing men, the wounded heart. We build men up to become the leaders God intended us to be, for Him, for our families and for the lost sheep out there. Most men in Warriors have their own church that they attend which is important. We need that discipleship and wisdom from the sermons the Preacher will speak to us.

The book – ACT LIKE MEN – written by James Macdonald, says one of the biggest hindrances to relationships among men is our tendency to hold things inside. We hide, and cover, and close ourselves off to the kind of openness that causes male friendships to flourish and faith in God to grow. You may be fearful of making yourself known. Possibly you are fearful or have been hurt, or learned to bottle up what you experience. Amazing things happen when men drop their guard and get honest with each other.

John 1:3-5 (NIV)
"Through Him all things were made; without Him nothing was made that has been made. In Him was life, and that life was the light of men. The light shines in the darkness, but the darkness has not understood it."

Do you ever feel that your life is too complex for God to understand? Remember, God created the entire universe, and nothing is too difficult for Him. God created you; He is alive today, and His love is bigger than any problem you may face. Not only will getting the wound out make you feel at peace, but your story will help other brothers come out and share theirs too. You will be amazed at how many brothers can relate to you and your story. When we share at camps with each other our stories or wounds, stay there. Our wounds and stories go in the dumpster, never to be brought up again. The tough part is forgiveness for the people who created those wounds in your life; it's very tough. But if we don't forgive those that hurt us, the Lord will not forgive us. Satan is sly, and he will bring up the past in our minds. He will remind us of our wounds, things we have done that we are not proud of. God does not bring up our past, some think He does, but once you ask for forgiveness and forgiveness for those who have hurt you in some way and truly mean it sincerely, God *never* brings it back up.

Hebrews 10:17 (NIV)
He then adds: "Their sins and lawless acts I will remember no more."

I hear people say they are not going to forgive him or her for what they did to me (the wound) until they hear the words "I'm sorry" to me first. There is a lot of hate in the world over our wounds, but I think about Jesus being crucified, the people that hated him, whipped him, beat him, and nailed Him to the cross to die. What Jesus went through; none of us will endure in our lifetime the kind of hate and pain that they inflicted upon Him. In turn, Jesus died for our sins, forgave those that gave Him such a beating, a beating that no other human today would survive. While He was nailed to the cross, Jesus said, "Father, forgive them as they know not what they are doing!" God knows every one of us, before we were even thought of in our mother's womb. The Lord knows our future, what lies ahead of us. He knows what we will go through in our lifetime. He knows the hardships, trials, the unknown that lies in front of all of us. He also knows the good times. If life went perfectly, we probably wouldn't think there was a God. But this is why we live amongst evil in the world. We make our choices that

God gave us. He gave us the choice to follow Him, to live by His Word and His standards. God gave all of us a story to share, the story of our life before we had a relationship with Him. The story of when we found Him and how He changed our life for the better.

Your testimony or story is a form of praise and honor to Christ. We also use it to encourage others. Know that every time you're going through trials and sufferings, that they become an opportunity to share a testimony of how God worked in your life and made you stronger.

Philippians 1:12 (NIV)
"Now I want you to know, brothers, that what has happened to me has really served to advance the gospel."

Being in W.A.H.M. now for thirteen years and all the camps I've been to, listening to all the stories shared from men, I have seemed to develop what I would call a gift from God. God guiding men into my path that are hurting, carrying a wound and just sitting there and talking to them and them sharing a little with me is amazing. I can tell from listening to them, the little they share, that they are guarding their heart, and I can tell they are carrying a wound deep down they want to get out but don't know how. With God at my side talking through me, I know I must be careful with what I say in order not to push them away. With love and God in our conversation we seem to connect and the next thing I know, they are sharing their story with me. What I am about to share with you about my story or testimony, as you may recall, it is in no way an attempt to hurt or make anyone look bad. The forgiveness has already been given and that part of my story is done. My love for my dad is strong. I have done a lot of praying on this section of my book and feel very strongly about sharing it with all of you. This is to show you where I was at and how a person can turn their life around with the love of Christ in your heart. My love for the Lord grows stronger every day.

2 Corinthians 5:17 (NIV)
"Therefore, if anyone is in Christ, he is a new creation; the old has gone, the new has come."

Around the second night of the Warrior Camp, I was sitting and listening to other brothers' testimonies, and I felt a knot in my stomach and weird feelings, some of the brothers call that the "Holy Spirit." I was scared and knew in my heart that I needed to get up front and share. When Randy said, "Who's next?" My hand went up and I was committed. What I love about these camps is we are never forced to do or say anything if we don't feel like it. It's our time there with God. God had a different plan for me that night and I knew I needed to share this wound. In my life, I made sure that no man or woman ever saw me shed a tear from feeling emotional. Not only did I shed a tear that night, but it was also like a flood! I thought to myself *Man what is wrong with me? I am bawling like a baby.* At that moment in my life, I realized how powerful God and the Holy Spirit were, working on me and how good it felt to let those emotions out after forty years. This is my wound. My brother, sister, and I lived with our mom, who was divorced from our dad. We were young and didn't know what was going on in our lives. Our mom, as I mentioned before, was an incredibly beautiful Scottish lady born in Dundee, Scotland. My Dad met her when he was stationed in Scotland. He married her there and my brother was born in Scotland. My Dad moved back to the states (with my mom and brother) where my sister and I were born. The brief time we lived with our mom was awesome. I still remember to this day her beautiful black hair and beautiful smile. Every time I look at my daughter Jessica with her beautiful black hair and same beautiful smile, I can see my mom in her. I remember my mom being so happy all the time, always telling us how much she loved us. I remember her singing Scottish songs to us and dancing. My favorite was, *you take the high road, I'll take the low road.*

Ephesians 4:32 (NIV)
"Be kind and compassionate to one another, forgiving each other, just as in Christ God forgave you."

My parents got divorced. My siblings and I didn't understand what was going on. We knew we were happy being with our mom and had a lot of great memories with her in the brief time we spent being with her. Our mom, over the divorce, had started drinking quite a bit and became an alcoholic. During the time she drank, she was never mean to us. I remember her just loving us every day. My mom didn't have many friends in the small town where we grew up. I was told outsiders from other countries weren't really accepted back then.

(Those who are unwilling to forgive have not become one with Christ, who was willing to forgive even those who crucified Him.)

Then came the day our world shattered, it is a little foggy in my mind, but I remember I was probably around eight years old, and my dad showed up at the house we lived in with our mom, loaded up my sister, my brother and myself and drove us away from the house. That was the last time I saw my mom until I was twenty-four years old. We were like a bunch of scared puppies being taken away from their home.

I remember pulling up to this old house which was a few doors down from our grandma. As we walked in, we met our soon-to-be stepmom for the first time. The first night in the bedroom felt like a prison, there were several bunk beds. I stayed on the bottom bunk along with my brother and sister. We also had three stepbrothers that we had never met, sharing the bunk beds. That was probably one of the longest nights of my life. Still, we were never told at that time why we were taken away from our mom, and we were too scared to ask.

Matthew 6:14-15 (NIV)
"For if you forgive men when they sin against you, your Heavenly Father will also forgive you. But if you do not forgive men their sins, your Father will not forgive your sins."

My siblings and I were told my mom didn't want us and that she sold us to our dad because she didn't love us. Later, in life, we found this out to be a lie and that my mom did want to see us, but our stepmom wouldn't let her. At one point, we were told that our stepmom had decided to let my mom come and take us for the weekend. The weekend came and she (our stepmom) took us to our cabin. She said it was the next weekend that our mom was coming to get us. The next weekend, our stepmom told us was the weekend my mom was coming to get us. We were so excited to see her and waited all weekend, but she never showed up. The truth was she had been there the weekend before as she was told that was her weekend to get us. My mom had waited at our house all weekend, but, of course, we weren't there. We never had any idea that our mom wanted to see us. My stepmom manipulated the whole thing; we thought our mom didn't want to see us and my mom thought the same thing. I really think it hurt my mom so badly that she started drinking more. Our stepmom told us our mom didn't love us because she never showed up to see us. We were heartbroken. Eventually, my mom moved away from Craig, Colorado, and we moved out to the country with a bigger house and some acreage, which I loved, because I didn't have to be around my stepmom that much. I loved playing sports, but if we didn't have anything to do after school, when we got home, my sister, brother, and I had to clean, and I mean clean, the entire house. She would have a big chalkboard with chores written down on it that we had to get done after school and if it wasn't, we got beat with a belt. Her three boys never had to do anything around the house when it came to chores. It wasn't the work that bothered me, we were willing to do whatever it took to keep the peace at home. Probably what I missed the most, looking back on my life, was there wasn't any love, comfort, or caring at all. We were scared to ask for lunch money for school and sometimes we would go days without eating until we got the nerve to ask for a few dollars. We learned not to complain to my dad, because he would confront her, which she would deny, then later take it out on us. (My dad was always gone with his work) We learned to live in fear and take the punches as we went. Even friends wouldn't come over because they knew what type of person she was. One day, I don't know what came over her, but she took me outside and beat me with the big end of an extension cord. I'll never figure that one out, she was probably just having a difficult day and I was the closest thing to take it out on. In all those years, I never heard a prayer said at the dinner

table or anywhere else in the house. At Christmas time, all I knew was that it was about presents. I never knew that it was the time to celebrate the birth of Jesus. We had to earn our own money and with the money I earned, I bought hay for my horse. My stepbrother had a horse also and she bought hay for him. The one thing I also remember is going out to our stepmom's parents ranch and spending time there. I loved it there and our stepmom's mom was one of the nicest ladies to be around, her love and caring flowed from her, which I loved. I could never understand how my stepmom could be so hateful and mean and her mom could be so loving. When it came time to start the new school year, our stepmom would take me shopping and with my hard-earned money, paying for my new clothes she would pick them out for me. I know she hated me, but I think she also wanted to embarrass me, anyway, I had no choice in the matter of what she picked out. I wanted regular cowboy boots, Wranglers, or Levi Jeans and she got just that. But the jeans were the biggest bell bottoms that could be found, the ones like all the long-haired hippies wore and the cowboy boots she picked out had the pointiest toes. I looked like I was wearing women's high heels.

My brother and I were always in each other's faces and picking on each other. Sibling rivalry, we were both missing something in our lives, and that was love from someone who cared for us. Anyway, one day, our stepmom had enough of our fighting and took us both outside, held a belt in her hand with the buckle end toward the ground, and told us to get it out of our system and that if we quit, we would get the belt. I would rather get beat to a pulp from my brother than to get that belt. So, we did just that, we beat each other senseless. With each punch, our hearts cried, but we had to keep going. What hurt me the deepest was my dad standing there, seeing all of it and never saying a word. I lost a lot of respect for my dad that night.

John 6:63 (NIV)

"The spirit gives life; the flesh counts for nothing. The words I have spoken to you are spirit and they are life."

(Footnotes)

The Holy Spirit gives spiritual life; without the work of the Holy Spirit, we cannot even see the need for new life. (14:17) All spiritual renewal begins and ends with God. He reveals the truth to us, lives within us, and then enables us to respond to that truth.

We couldn't wait for the day we grew up. When we grew stronger and bigger, we stood up for ourselves and our stepmom knew that she couldn't control or take advantage of us like she did when we were younger. We still lived in fear but did our chores and tried to stay out of her way. Up until I graduated from High School, nothing was ever brought up about our mom and we never asked.

There did come a time when we were reunited with my mom after we moved to Grand Junction, Colorado. I was married with small children and one day, we got a call from a local nursing home. The nurse that called me told me one of her patients kept telling her she had a son named Jeff Rippy and asked me if my mom was in a nursing home. At first, I was in shock and didn't know if they had confused me with someone else. They told me her birth name and everything about her and I knew that it had to be my mom. Kim and I went to see her, and it was a blessing to be reunited with my mom after all those years. In turn, it broke my heart, her being in a rest home and seeing what had become of my mom. At the same time, it also brought me immense joy to see her smile again, feeling her love and bringing back great memories of the brief time we got to spend with her at an early age.

The years we had with my mom (after we found her in the nursing home) were precious times, both going to see her and bringing her to our home. She had the opportunity to spend time with her grandchildren and with Kim and me. She loved elk meat, mashed potatoes, and gravy. Kim made that dinner every time we brought her home, it was her favorite. I really must give a lot of credit (like always) to Kim for always pushing me to go see my mom. My mom was always so excited when we showed up. I asked Kim one day, "How do you think my mom found us?" Kim with her smile said, "It was all God."

The day came when we got the call that mom was on her death bed. Kim and I went to the rest home, walked into my mom's room, and saw her laying there smiling and talking away while staring up at the ceiling. I looked at the nurse who had a big smile on her face and tears running down her cheeks and asked her, "What is she saying? I can't understand her." The nurse looked at Kim and me and said with a smile, "She sees her parents at a young age and wants to go with them to Heaven." We all had tears streaming from sadness, but also tears of happiness, knowing mom was going to be in a better place with our Heavenly Father. I leaned down to Mom and she said, "I have been waiting for you, Jeff, I have always loved you."

Psalm 16:10 (NIV)

"Because you will not abandon me to the grave, nor will you let your Holy One see decay. You have made known to me the path of life; you will fill me with joy in your presence, with eternal pleasures at your right hand."

I hugged her and told her, "I love you too mom, it's Ok, go home to Jesus." Mom passed on that night. We had her cremated and I had her box of ashes for several years not knowing what to do with them. One day it hit me, burying her ashes at Camp Red Cloud in Lake City, Colorado. That's where my life changed, where I came to know Jesus, where I faced the wound from my childhood and found forgiveness for my stepmom and dad. God was immensely powerful up there and helped me realize how blessed I was to have my mom back in my life for the time I did. With the help of several brothers, we saddled our horses and picked a beautiful place, in God's creation, and celebrated my mom's time here on earth, but most importantly, we celebrated my mom being in Heaven.

Psalm 63:3-4 (NIV)
"Because your love is better than life, my lips will glorify you. I will praise you as long as I live, and in your Name I will lift up my hands."

God has a plan for every one of us whether you know it or not. The day you were thought of in your mother's womb, God knew your future and where or how your life on this earth would go. But God gave each of us choices to make, whether we walk with Him or away from Him. The choice is yours, make the right choice to follow God and invite Him into your daily lives. Believe me, it's fun and worth it, and is extremely rewarding.

Live The Code Of The West In Such A Way People Will Come To Know God, Because They Know You

Matthew 5:16 (NIV)

"In the same way, let your light shine before men, that they may see your good deeds and praise your Father in heaven."

They say: Actions speak louder than words. I once heard a preacher say, "No such thing as an accident, you were born for a purpose. If you never discover your value, you won't discover your purpose." It is easy for us to look good in church or other religious events. But when we walk out those doors of church, it becomes the real test of how people really see us, how we act around strangers, or at home and work. Like I said, we can all look good at church, but there is another side to a lot of people once they walk out of those doors. That's what a lot of non-Christians call hypocrites, which gives believers a bad name. Several years ago, I asked a question at a church breakfast, "Brothers, are we living our lives outside of the church doors the way that Christ would want us to? Bringing brothers and sisters closer to Him?" Everyone kind of looked at me and agreed with me. We have people in the church that are Christ followers, but there are still some in church we need to work with and pray for. People, the church is outside those doors and our job as Christians and God's disciples is to reach out to them. The way to do this is to show Christ's love through ourselves and God will do the rest.

2 Corinthians 4:7 (NIV)
"But we have this treasure in jars of clay to show that this all-surpassing power is from God and not from us."

God uses us to spread His good news and He gives us the power to do His work. Knowing that the power is His, not ours, should keep us from pride and motivate us to keep daily contact with Him, our power source. Our responsibility is to let people see God through us.

Back before my walk grew strong with God, I really was not the one that people would come to Christ because they knew me. I really wasn't a bad person, but I wasn't bringing them to Christ. I was a very lukewarm Christian. It wasn't until things in me changed and my walk, along with my love for the Lord, grew stronger every day. Did my life get easier? NO! But it did get better with Gods love in my heart and knowing my propose in life, building an even stronger relationship with God to where brothers and sisters would see the love of Christ through me, while giving God all the glory, Amen.

Actions Speak Louder Than Words

Proverbs 2:6 (NIV)
"For the Lord gives Wisdom, and from His mouth come knowledge and understanding."

You are no such thing as an accident, you were born for a purpose. If you never discover your value, you won't discover your purpose.

I really like the quote: "Actions speak louder than words." How true this is as Christians today. We are living up to God's standards through the eyes of Christians and Non-Christians by our actions in society outside the church doors, but of course, we all look good inside those doors. I like the quote a friend sent me a while back, it says, "It's all about what you do when no one is watching."

I would like to share some stories with you about how people can see God's light shine through you in your actions. Back in August of 2014, I went to North Dakota for a job consulting on a work-over-rig completing gas wells. As I was driving up there, with the sixteen-hour drive ahead of me, I was questioning God as to why He was sending me there. I was not at all excited about going to this job that far away from home.

Matthew 5:16 (NIV)

"In the same way, let your light shine before men, that they may see your good deeds and praise your Father in Heaven."

Later in life, I would realize I shouldn't have been questioning God on why He was taking me so far away. What I should have done was ask God, "What can I do for your Kingdom up here?" Sometimes our plans are not God's plans. He knows what is best for us and puts us in that place or position to do His work. After work, the first day I was signing the rig ticket and my Rig operator Curtis, who was a big husky young man, looked at me and said, "You don't mind if I ask you a personal question do you?" "Not at all," I replied. He looked me square in the eyes and asked, "Are you religious?" I was a little shocked and taken back by the question of being in the oilfield and all. I never had any religious markings on me or my truck nor did I bring up God that day.

Matthew 5:20 (NIV)
"For I tell you that unless your righteousness surpasses that of the Pharisees and the teachers of the law, you will certainly not enter the Kingdom of Heaven."

(Footnotes)

God judges our hearts as well as our deeds, for it is in the heart that our real allegiance lies. But just as concerned about our attitudes that people don't see, as about your actions that are seen by all.

I looked at Curtis straight back into his eyes and said, "Yes, I have a relationship with the Lord, why do you ask?" "We thought so." He said, "We never heard one cuss word out of your mouth all day long and that is not normal for a Company man, and we were betting with each other if you were religious or not." While I was standing there smiling and thinking to myself, *Okay Lord, this is what it's about, spreading your Name and giving you all the glory.* Right then, Curtis broke my train of thought when he asked me, "Do we offend you with our bad mouths, cussing up a storm?"

I looked over at Curtis and his crew. "No, that is not for me to judge, that's the Lord's job." I went ahead to tell them that, "Quite a few years ago, they couldn't hold a candlestick to my mouth, it was every other word that was a cuss word coming out of my mouth." The Lord was watering the seed that day and the whole Rig crew received (NIV) Cowboy Bibles. Several days later, we were having issues on the well and I was standing back on the edge of the location just checking the issue out. Curtis came up to me and asked me, "Do you mind if I ask you another question?" I said, "Not at all, what's on your mind?" With that confused look in his eye, he asked, "What is it about you? I can't figure you out. I have never met anyone like you before. Here we are having issues on this well and you're as calm as can be. Most company men would be yelling, cussing, and stressed out. What is it about you?"

Looking back at him I said "You know Curtis, I still stress out, I'm human, but in the years with my walk with God, I've learned to give my worries to Him. That's what He is here for to guide us and give us wisdom and strength." Curtis looked at me, smiled, and said, "You know. My family is religious, but me I kind of fell away from God, maybe I should get back into my walk with Him.," I looked at Curtis and told him, "You know that's your choice and only yours to start your walk with God. But promise me one thing if you do get your relationship going again with God that you will not try to do it alone. Find a brother to do the walk together with, otherwise it won't work."

Ecclesiastes 4:9-10 (NIV)
"Two are better than one, because they have a good return for their work: If one falls down, his friend can help him up. But pity the man who falls and has no one to help him up!"

When my time was up to leave that job and go on to another adventure, I could see a difference in Curtis. God was watering that seed in his life.

This adventure really opened my eyes to how other people watch you in life and can see the kind of person you are by your actions. That opens the door to sharing the word of Jesus and to planting that seed. God will water it and grow it step by step.

Back in the '90's, I was visiting with a close friend of mine who was a Police Officer in a small town. As we were visiting, he told me that before he became a Police Officer, he knew everyone in town and would see them downtown or at a public event and how they were great people to be around. Then he went on to tell me that once he became a police officer and had calls to some of the more respectable people's homes, it was like night and day. People live different lives behind closed doors. A life my Cop friend wouldn't brag about. A life that wouldn't lead other men to God. I think sometimes, we don't think about anyone knowing what we are doing behind those doors. But God sees, He sees everything we do and eventually will reveal it to the outside. I was there at a time in my life. As I said earlier in the book, I was one of the biggest posers around. But being around men during that time in my life, that were Godly men with their leadership qualities, character, love, and good will, I wanted what these men had, their love for our Father, and our Savior Jesus Christ. It all comes down to taking that first step, brothers and sisters. Give God the reigns to your life, only you can make that choice. Us men seem to hold onto our pride and try being the tough man. That was me. Once I gave God my life and started living by His standards, life got so much better, along with my marriage. Is life free of troubles and worries? No! This is an evil and corrupt world we live in, but knowing when it's my time to go, I'll be in Heaven with our loving Father for eternity. Remember brothers and sisters, we have a crucial decision in this world. Heaven or Hell. Make the right choice, it's never too late. Love you and God Bless

Praying Cowboy

Conclusion

The writing of this book, which took over two years to finish, was both enjoyable and touching. My love for the Lord and my marriage is stronger than it has ever been. From the book – You and Me Forever – (Most marriage problems are not really marriage problems. They are God problems. They can be traced back to one or both couples having poor relationships with God or a faulty understanding of Him.) How true that this is.

My prayer is that this book gets to the lost sheep out there and that my story will bring them closer to Christ. With God as my guide writing the words in here, I look for no fame or fortune. God gets the glory of this book.

I want to thank my beautiful wife Kim for all her support and for always believing in me during the tough times.

Thank you to my four grown adult kids for their love, and support, and for always believing in the old man.

Thanks to my mother and father-In-Law, Sue and Newt for their prayers, and their love and for helping me build the foundation of God in my life.

Thank you, God, for blessing me with my dad, and how his heart has opened to you.

Thank you to the rest of the family and especially my Brother-In-Law Sean for showing me what a Godly man lives like and for inviting me to my first Warrior at Heart Ministry Breakfast back in 2006. Without that invite, this book would never have been in the making. Thanks to all the Warrior at Heart brothers for their love, prayers, encouragement, and support all these years.

Thanks to my preacher Chris Coleman and his lovely family for their support, love, and friendship. A brother whom I look up to on his teachings about the Lord and who helped build the foundation of Christ in my life.

I also want to thank Ed and Lori Currey who supported me in the writing of this book. Special thanks to Lori who volunteered to take the rough draft and put it onto the computer, spending countless hours and days of challenging work to get the book to what it is.

Most of all, I thank God our Father for His love and the many blessings, and the blessings yet to come, for every one of us. My prayer is that every one of you will come close to Christ and spend eternity with Him.

GOD BLESS PRAYING COWBOY

Notes

Prayers & Answers to Prayers

Notes

Prayers & Answers to Prayers

Notes

Prayers & Answers to Prayers

Notes

Prayers & Answers to Prayers

Notes

Prayers & Answers to Prayers

www.ingramcontent.com/pod-product-compliance
Ingram Content Group UK Ltd.
Pitfield, Milton Keynes, MK11 3LW, UK
UKHW021909190726
13853UKWH00002B/589